AGENDA

CONTENTS

Introduction: Patricia McCarthy	
POEMS	
Johnny Marsh: Spring Sonnet	10
John Greening: *Variations on a Ghazal*	11
Mimi Khalvati: *Ghazal*	12
AlFresco	13
John F. Deane: *Lucy in the Sky*	14
Grandmother	15
John Kinsella: *Solomon Icon*	16
David Cooke: *Under Cygnus*	17
Robert Stein: *We Do Not Speak of This*	19
Winter	19
Moon Poem	20
Michael Kirkham: *Night Thoughts*	21
Michael Hamburger: *Towards Equanimity*	22
Jay Parini: *Borges in Scotland*	24
Peter Dale: *Kids' Game*	25
Heugh	25
W.S. Milne: *'Over you now the wild winds blow'*	26
Harry Guest: *Florum Imagines*	27
Sam Gardiner: *Nursery Walks*	29
Ian Caws: *Requiem for a Downland Shepherd*	30
André Frénaud: *I have never forgotten you*	31
Translated by William Oxley	
Ángelos Sikelianós: *Acrocorinth*	32
Doric	33
The Garden at Mistrá	33
Translated by Timothy Adès	
Güven Turan: *Poem to Snow on the Way*	35
Translated by Ruth Christie	

1

ESSAYS/REVIEWS

W.S. Milne: *The Poetry of Nessie Dunsmuir* — 37
Greg Delanty: poem: *The New Voyager* — 47
Daniel Tobin: *World Music: The Collected Poems of Greg Delanty* — 48
Eavan Boland: poem: *Becoming the Hand of John Speed* — 55
Tony Roberts: *Eavan Boland: New and Collected Poems* — 56

TWO POEMS INSPIRED BY JOHN CLARE

Robert Etty: *I kicked it out of the clods* — 65
Robert Hamberger: *Heading North* (part of a sequence) — 66

ESSAYS

Edward Ragg: *Abstraction and its Detractors: Wallace Stevens in the 21st Century* — 74
Edward Ragg: poem inspired by Wallace Stevens: *Owl and Cat* — 80
Robert Stein: *What should Modern Poetry do?* — 81

SEQUENCE OF POEMS

John Haynes: *Spirit Possession* — 86

REVIEWS

Duncan Sprott: *Time Stopped: recent poetry of Thomas McCarthy, John Seed and translations of C.P. Cavafy* — 89
Michael Kinsella: *Nothing to communicate, thankfully: Nick Laird: To a Fault* — 94

POEMS

Alison Brackenbury: *The Shell* — 96
Solo — 96
Enclosed — 97
Malcolm MacClancy: *Réalta* — 98
Geraldine Paine: *You were too Young* — 99

Linda Saunders: *Dipper*	100
Kelims in Stoke Newington	102
Stuart Henson: *The River at Rodmell*	103
Heather Coffey: *Beating the Bounds*	105
Tom MacIntyre: *She*	106
Scissors	106
Tania van Schalkwyk: *My Grandmother's Art*	107
Viv Apple: *Father Figure*	108
Mark Leech: *The Beast*	110
Judith Kazantzis: *In Rome*	111
Mark Harris: *A Century of Sounds: The Fork*	112
Pneumoconiosis (Black Lung Disease)	113
Richard Marggraf Turley: *Afterlives*	114
Debouching	115
Matthew Geden: *Ghosts*	116
Gracious Networks	116
Sally Lucas: *Recitation*	117
Lisa Dart: *Annunciation*	118

CHOSEN YOUNG BROADSHEET POET

Simon Pomery: *Anima*	119
Uncle Rodge	119
The Folksinger	120
Send no Flowers	121
Broadsheet 7 online: www.agendapoetry.co.uk	121

NOTES FOR BROADSHEET POETS 7:   122

Peter Abbs: *The Four Tasks of the Contemporary Poet*	123
Steven O'Brien: *Songs and Dreams as Sources of Poetry*	132

POEMS

John Fuller: *How Far?* 137

Caroline Price: *Messages* 139
The Alde at Snape 140

Clive Wilmer: poems: *A Blue Tit's Egg, Learning to Read, and Translator's Apology* 141

Iain Britton: *At the site of the future I light a fire ...* 142
Ourselves Written in Wood 144

Susan Wicks: *Cat's Eye, Soft Shoulder* 145
What do we do with Spring? 146
French Kissing in Brittany 146
Stained Glass 147

Lynn Roberts: *Adonis* 148

Pat Earnshaw: *Puppet without Strings* 149

Myra Schneider: *Strawberries* 152

Nicholas Jagger: *Das Nachtlied* 152

Moya Cannon: *Starlings* 153

Mc. Donald Dixon: *Three Palms at Commerette* 154

BIOGRAPHIES 156

Front cover illustration:

Nancy Wynne-Jones was born in Dolgellau, North Wales in 1922. Her studies at the Royal Academy of Music were cut short by the war. These studies were not not resumed. After the war, instead of returning to music, she turned to painting. She studied painting at Heatherly's; Chelsea College of Art, and with Peter Lanyon in St. Ives, where she settled for many years. In 1972 she moved to Ireland where she still lives and works.

In the 1980s she began composing again, writing several small orchestral pieces which complemented her painting with their landscaped themes; these were publicly performed. This excerpt is from one of them: Prismatics, for 14 instruments.

INTRODUCTION

Welcome to another single issue of *Agenda* which shows the rich diversity in poets mainly from England, Wales, Scotland and Ireland, but also from New Zealand (Iain Britton) and St Lucia (Mc. Donald Dixon). Along with well-known poets long associated with *Agenda* such as Peter Dale, former Associate Editor of *Agenda*, Michael Hamburger, Harry Guest, Clive Wilmer, Robert Stein, John Greening and Sam Milne, there is a wealth of fresh established voices such as the Australian poet, John Kinsella, described by Martin Dodsworth in the Australian issue as a 'genius of sorts', Eavan Boland and Greg Delanty, both of Irish origin and both of whose *Collected Poems* have recently come out from Carcanet, John Deane, founding editor of the Dedalus Press and of Aosdána, whose poetry has featured in *Agenda* in recent years, Alison Brackenbury, Mimi Khalvati who runs the Poetry School in London. William Oxley, Michael Kirkham, Ian Caws and David Cooke are names you will recognise from former issues, as well as the fine translator of Turkish (see *Agenda*'s Turkish issue, Vol. 38 Nos. 3–4), Ruth Christie. The latter is joined here by Timothy Adès with his translations from the Greek and whose translations/versions of further poems by Jean Cassou, the little known French Resistance poet (following on from his *33 Sonnets of the Resistance*, published by Arc), it is hoped, will be published by **Agenda Editions**.

There are two sequences, or parts of sequences, which have deliberately been inserted separately so that they can have their own space in which to be absorbed as they continue *Agenda*'s tradition of giving room to longer poems. One of them, by Robert Hamberger, concerns John Clare, and is accompanied by another single poem by Robert Etty on John Clare. The other part-sequence of unusual sonnets, by John Haynes, contains African influences.

Exciting new voices are here and I leave you to discover those for yourselves. Two first generation British poets, of Irish origin, also appear: Simon Pomery, the **chosen young Broadsheet poet**, age 23, born and brought up in the Republic of Ireland, but now resident in Derbyshire, having read English at the University of Leeds; and Steven O'Brien whose first collection, *Dark Hill Dreams*, was brought out this year by **Agenda Editions**. Steven shows, in the prose piece he contributes as part of the ongoing series: **Notes for Broadsheet Poets**, how strong an influence on his own poetry has been the singing of old national songs of deportees and emigrants in Irish pubs by his grandfather and uncle, and then himself. Eavan Boland explains, in her very poetically and articulately written book of prose *Object Lessons*, (Carcanet Press, 1995), how the dispossessed Irish nation, in the eighteenth and nineteenth centuries, became 'freighted with invention' which materialised in the songs and ballads of these centuries. Like O'Brien (and myself), she admits to loving these songs as both a child, a teenager, and even as an adult, seeking them out for their wonderful, terrible and memorable 'makeshift angers'. For the best of them were written – 'like the lyrics of Wyatt and Raleigh – within sight of the gibbet'. Yet, as she states, far from being 'entertainment', these songs proposed 'for the nation an impossible task: to be at once an archive of defeat and a diagram of victory'.

I attended the same English convent school as Eavan Boland, in Killiney, Co. Dublin, and remember learning to sing, unaccompanied, to a tuning fork, the black steps of notes of the Gregorian Chant; and going to tea with John McCormack's grandchildren in the house whose chapel had stained glass windows where the famous tenor had lived. His sonorous voice rang out from a crackling 'His Master's Voice' record on a gramophone over the grating of our roller skates in the surrounding little streets in Booterstown and over the more lyrical whispering of the sea's Joycean rhythms to Sandymount Strand.

Song itself is part of this issue. It not only unites the above-mentioned poets who all have their own unique pulse and tunes, whether formal or composed originally in their inner ear; it also celebrates, in retrospect, the work of the meditative American poet, Wallace Stevens, a poet not sufficiently recognised on this side of the Atlantic, probably because, as Frank Kermode, noted: he was so profoundly American, with a very un-English sensibility and he illustrates, as I found when I lived in the U.S., how very different American English is to English English or to Irish English, although ostensibly the same language. Yet, in his adoption of French, he stated, as Samuel Beckett could well have done, 'French and English constitute a single language' – and in the very music of his poetry, he can be read by us now as neither American nor English, nor European, but universal. Listen to how he sings, in his own distinctive voice, for example, about song:

> She was the single artificer of the world
> In which she sang. And when she sang, the sea,
> Whatever self it had, became the self
> That was her song, for she was the maker. Then we,
> As we beheld her striding there alone,
> Knew that there never was a world for her
> Except the one she sang, and singing, made.
> (from 'The Idea of Order at Key West')

This issue also demonstrates the gifts of an extremely fine Scots poet, Nessie Dunsmuir, wife of W.S. Graham, who has a clutch of merely ten poems extant (finely produced in a pamphlet by The Greville Press, 1988), but these poems, as Sam Milne demonstrates in his essay, are so supremely achieved that they deserve much greater attention. That such a consummate poet only produced ten poems begs the question: what happened to the rest? Were they deliberately destroyed for not being considered her finest, or was she – as Tony Astbury of the Greville Press, who knew her, implies – so fulfilled and consummated in her own being through the love between herself and her husband, that she had no need to write any more? The celebratory and rare art of 'being' in the moment perhaps over-rode any sense of achievement that her poems could offer. W.S. Graham's *Collected Poems* will be reviewed in the next issue.

And this leads to what poems actually do offer both to their authors and to readers. There is no doubt that the reader, while contributing his/her own experience of life, of other poems read, expectation even of what, for him/her constitutes 'poetry' and specific demands of the poet in question, lifts the poem off the page where it has already been given away by the poet, and makes it his or her own. In this way, the poem becomes a different poem to each reader and therefore has not only multiple forms but multiple meanings. The reader, thus, is also a creator, often carrying the melody of the poem in his/her head and releasing it into the world's echo-chamber. There is, in fact, an inherent blurring of roles between writers, readers and critics. After all, writers are their own critics and readers; readers are creators and critics, and critics are creators and readers. In academic circles that only too frequently expound theories of theories on specialised minutiae in a hermetic jargon, and continue to clarion, as George Steiner proclaims, 'the triumph of the theoretical', it must be stressed that it is the centrality of the text that *Agenda* continues to promote in its critical essays. It is the text that matters and must not be lost sight of, the text that is enlightened and illuminated by critics for readers who are then tempted to search out the text concerned and make it their own.

George Steiner continues, 'To read well is to be read by that which we read. It is to be answerable to it'. He goes on to say that there still attaches 'a fragrance of grace' to those who treat books as sacred'. R.S. Thomas, who, in his sparse, honed, lived-in lines, railed against the destruction in our world of the sense of sacrament, would have welcomed book-lovers with that 'fragrance of grace', even if the 'grace' be pagan.

Wallace Stevens defined what he meant for the full modern reality that he strove for in his singing by borrowing a phrase from Simone Weil who spoke of 'a reality of decreation in which our revelations are not the revelations of belief, but the precious portents of our own powers'. This is affirmed in Wallace Stevens' lines: 'The freshness of transformation is / The freshness of a world. It is our own, / It is ourselves, the freshness of ourselves'. It is this very 'freshness ourselves' that we all, whether writers or readers, wish to achieve in an increasingly violent, hedonistic world.

Stevens, who seemed on the whole to be in love with the world, was intent on giving 'pleasure' through his poetry which he fashioned as a savouring of life, a celebration. He even wanted poetry to restore health, to offer consolation, to mitigate poverty of the spirit, and unhappiness – all of which are laudable, humanistic, even social aims.

John Deane, however, in his interesting, very recently published book of prose, *In Dogged Loyalty, The Religion of Poetry: The Poetry of Religion* (Columbia Press, Dublin) does not settle for a poetry that merely gives 'pleasure'. This is no orthodox, bible-thumping book, but an impassioned plea in particular for a poetry that grasps 'the timeless out of the temporal', that 'delves into questions of transcendence' and argues 'against nothingness' so that 'mankind can still rise above its own bathetic self'. He cites the unlearneded loner, John Clare, (see the poems inspired by the latter in this issue) who, in his powerful, lyrical verse, stood out strongly against the prevailing materialism of his time, as we should all do while we share in 'this good fellowship of dust'. 'If poetry is reduced to serving the needs of amusement, the loss to the human spirit is immense. Poetry pushes experiences that are inaccessible to rational disquisition; it works to lift the rationalist into the shocking position of dealing with things that go bump beyond the thin partition of human reasoning'.

Like Wallace Stevens, John Deane is drawn to Simone Weil's thesis that redemption of sinful man is possible by 'reduction and annihilation of the ego, by "decreation"'. But, as Simone Weil discovered, this 'decreation' is impossible for the human will, although she did suggest that, like the mystics, a human creature can progress by moving away from the self to become empty, 'nothing'. Deane sees a saving grace in the poetry that articulates the inarticulate and 'provides the reader with a wider, deeper and more cumulative ordering that is vital to our understanding of the world'. He would concur with Peter Abbs whose essay 'The Four Tasks of the Contemporary Poet' I have chosen as the **Notes for Broadsheet Poets** in this issue. I quoted from Peter Abbs' equally impassioned and important book *Against the Flow: Education, The Arts and Post Modern Culture* (FalmerRoutledge) in the Celebratory issue for William Cookson Vol. 39 No. 4. John Deane has similar sentiments about musical poems rising above the mundane and popular polemic and transforming themselves into meanings beyond ordinary meanings. Deane also urges the importance of going 'against the flow': 'A poem is an epiphany, interrupting the flow'... The life of poetry will depend on whether or not we wish to have that flow interrupted'.

Fitting, perhaps, to round off these ruminations with a quote, first, from Wallace Stevens who refers to the role of the poet in Stalinist Russia: 'His role, in short, is to help people to live their lives'. This might not be a bad rule of thumb for all poets writing today. Eavan Boland declared, perhaps, on behalf of all of us in 'Object Lessons', 'I want a poem I can grow old in. I want a poem I can die in', even though she appreciated the difficulty for the poet in achieving such poems. In *Real Presences*, George Steiner states: 'Great poetry is, very exactly, that in which this homeward soughing of the musical tide is made to enrich, to deepen, the life of the word. A true poem, a live prose, a philosophic movement wholly consonant to its syntax, is one in which Odysseus sets observant words to the Sirens' song'.

A living 'Siren', Eavan Boland, then, must have the last word. In her telling poem 'The Singers', she describes the women on the 'unforgiving coast' of the West of Ireland whose mouths, at night, 'filled with / Atlantic storms and clouded-over stars / and exhausted birds',

> And only when the danger
> was plain in the music could you know
> their true measure of rejoicing in
>
> finding a voice where they found a vision.

Patricia McCarthy, October, 2006

Next double issue: *A Reconsideration of Rilke*, plus general section
Early spring, 2007

Visit the website www.agendapoetry.co.uk for online **Broadsheet 7**, further supplements to the magazine, news and history of *Agenda*.

Get a friend to subscribe and receive a free back issue of your choice (subject to availability).

Johnny Marsh

Spring Sonnet

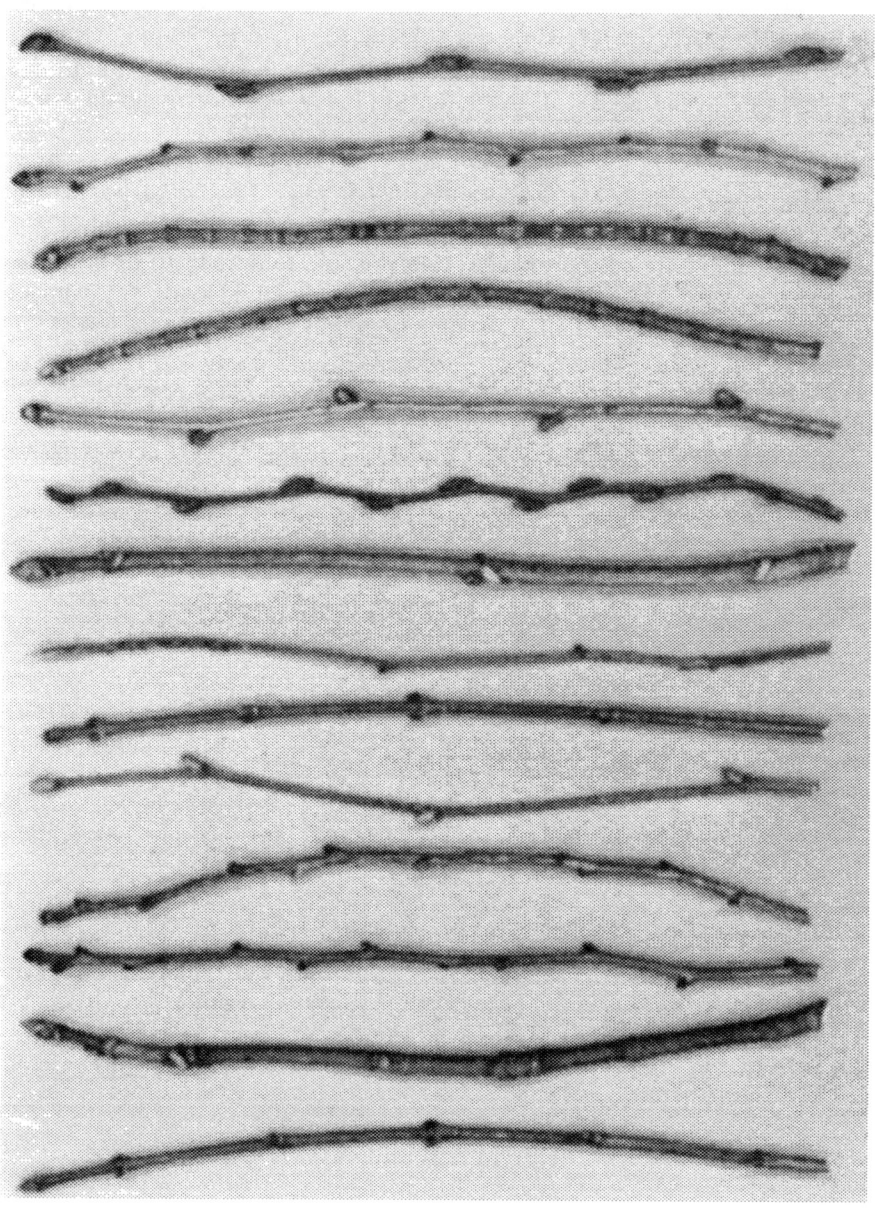

John Greening

Variations on a Ghazal

What is music? A sculpture carved out of air.
A counterpoint of earth, water, fire in the air.

It eats into the barnacled hull of work and pay,
drawing out its gold-fingered wire from the air.

Collar and veil and cocoon of a flame that converts
touchpaper lives to its pyre. It's the air

that the clay on bootsoles wishes for when it urges
our feet more slowly, much higher, where the air

is only fit for spheres. Music is the seed
within such bubble inspirations that aspire on the air,

then burst into canopy. It is a figured fermenting
in our cellars, the progress of Gaia through the air

to demijohn, a greening of black ashbuds, when all
sobriety and sackcloth vows expire to the air.

Mimi Khalvati

Ghazal

The bowling clouds have blown away,
bad birds of omen flown away.

Time is a house of many rooms
whose paper walls I've thrown away.

I've brushed the cobwebs, waved my wand,
djinn have driven my phone away.

So minions, come, and bring my love.
Love's but a stepping-stone away.

But when did love ever steal a march,
clear vines long overgrown away?

Love never even stole my sight
where blindness might have shown a way.

Pariya, come, and weave your song,
wave every devil you've known away.

Sing in my name and in my heart
before I give my own away.

pariya: fairies

AlFresco

Look – there's the thrips on the daisy
too small to see, the spangle galls
on oak, the Noonday-fly on walls
basking in my insectary!

And what are these – millipedes? –
strewing the ground like broken springs
while cicadas whistle, crickets sing,
harvester ants sit husking seeds.

Horsefly, housefly, scorpion, bee,
wasps that drowned in the pool but flew,
rosemary flowers I forgot were blue,
I salute you, hesitantly.

Here's ham for you, melon and cheese,
tortillas, tarts, to your heart's content
and for you, mosquito, bent
on blood, gallons to drink as you please.

Summer's on the wing. So, earwig,
locust, beetle and bug, spoil yourselves,
don't stint. Once we've flown you can delve
in dung, in rubble topped with figs.

But when night falls on the floodlit hill,
lacewing, chafer, beware that glass!
Not every window will let you pass.
One light is all it takes to kill.

John F. Deane

Lucy in the Sky

They have gone down into old earth
to prepare their motorways and have discovered

bones; yellow big-engines with their jaws and angers
move in sway-time on a scaffolding of skulls; like sods

of dried-out turf, the scapulas of biped hominids
are unearthed; what makes us human, we are told, is laughter

and walking upright. Pithecus, and Peking Man Erectus,
and they found Lucy, of Ethiopia, one forearm bone

reaching from the soil, forty percent of her
raised skywards in tentative resurrection. And you, the Christ,

they raised you skywards and hammered you in,
bones stretched and shattered on the hill of skulls,

they put you under earth where we, too, marginalia,
will lay us down inside the calcium honeycombs, longside

the Jesus body, the Jesus bones. Resurrections that a slight
contemporary breeze might whisk out of our seeing.

Set Lucy upright, cautiously, dust out the orifices
of heard melodies, of sand-marrow; clean between the teeth

and snuff dust out from the nostrils; think of eyes that have absorbed
the light of summers, of a brain that has stored truths and trivia,

language and languages and a modicum of history. You will find
nothing of that. Dust carefully the bones; perhaps the Christ

has already raked them through, rifling what's left
for garnered treasures. Take care, too, with the skull, the jaw askew

in mocking laughter. Who she was, or is, or if she watches still,
she is indifferent to your amorous tickling of her bones.

Grandmother

We stood and dared not whisper. All about the room
the intensity of candle-flame and the terrible stillness
of white flowers; I could imagine it, original storm,

darkness and the unnamed noises, and how the structure
of all created things was in fearful flux: the core
like a porridge stirred by thunders and spirit-shattering lightnings,

the surfaces as molten lava. In the sick-room the loved old woman
was lying motionless save where the lips were offering
inaudible whispers; there was a tiny silver crucifix

dipped in blessed water and I was figuring
Jesus harrowing her where all of heaven and earth
was splitting apart within her, the spirit moving back

out of the ordered waters, the flesh, the flesh
appetites, the disappointments and she was faring out
on unbearable waves of fire, time's shackles and our tears

inhibiting, the way we held her small hooked hand, the way
we laid soft cloths across her brow; how she must cast us
off and cast time off and burn forever in that healing fire.

John Kinsella

Solomon Icon

For us, beneath the wandoo of Mount Observation national park;
    there you stood upright, facing the glowing bark,
    there a slow fertility worked its way through years, countries.

When the night birds fail to illuminate the dark let me replace your sight,
    let me replace your hearing;
my love is stronger than the seen or the heard,
    it burns hotter than lightning.

The cascading emptiness than pins you down
    is uplifted by atomic heat: suns burn where your eyes, your ears
    were.

Floods of loss and bleakness and death-wish stronger than sunset
    cannot wash away the love I've implanted.

No amount of experimentation or hypothesising will bring more knowledge
    than love given when the night birds find the night too dark to fly.

David Cooke

Under Cygnus

Midnight among the Roman ruin
Where the earth itself is thin –
Along these strata take a walk,
Speak theology, yet the talk,
Like the oracle, does not illumine –
Its priests are dying in their bed.
Gone their mosaic lettering
Which told the living of the dead,
Whose statues fall – are falling
To where each forgets their origin.

Look up, look up – a constellation
Beats its wings, night is strong, dreams
Forbid the Emperor to foretell
The cost is borne by dying well.
Life here is beyond our means,
Only ghosts guest a banquet meal.
The *lost ones* arrive here in spring,
They whisper: *You are not real
But idling on ground long given
To burial of the dying.*

The heroic age dips quietly by.
Garden statues move and sigh:
He is not here, he is gone.
Gone the symmetry, the clipped
Hedgerow, the marble statesmen
Who leave in formal procession,
Carrying their togas through the arched
Colonnade – gone the pool where narcissi
Bloomed, where, among such statuary,
Ornamental fish politely swam.

At beat of wings the statues fall,
Fear and darkness here vacate,
Yet like these ruins they await
To enact their hour and recall

Where the marble men are gone.
Midnight knows of no control -
Only two herons on patrol
Call and ghost and falling scan
These walls with rain drumming on
The muffled wing-beats of the *Swan*.

Robert Stein

We Do Not Speak of This

It is a language even the illiterate know,
That the blind can read easily – the freehand
Of leaves caught and flustered through the air,
The scribble of weeds at the water's edge,
The foreign characters I have hurriedly put
On the other side of this page.

The spoor of what we might be
Lurks in the corner of each eye –
The face we might have known,
The car we almost didn't see,
The night ice, the loneliness
Sliding towards us
In the heltering playground of the rain.

Winter

Endless silence falling with the snow.
The man across the fields is the first man
And this the new world.
The birds re-name themselves as on they go.

I think of heaven like this -
Like a field of gentle snow –
Like rejoicing stars and calm star-light;
Like nothing that is.

You whom I loved have taken yourself away
And called me guilty. Suffering is what you do best.
Your picture stares at me from the East.
Your wrong love hurts me every day.

So my heart is white and silent like the damned
And you do not answer from your cross,
The world heavy on your broken shoulders,
Blood on your unmoved hands.

Moon Poem

I am calling to my father now,
He glances up somewhere – from hammering,
From his desk, from sleeping, from praying –
As a child he'd hold me up against the angel moon.
I picture his huge face by a light, still wondering.

I am calling also to my mother who is angry
At me, my father, the evening sky,
The beasts of the constellations, their fixed answering.
In her voice I hear leaves falling.
An unearthly spider has crawled across her heart.

My brother, an athlete, I love him.
There is a scar on his arm where he fell, losing.
He breaks the tape but the tape holds him back.
Something pulls at the stream of his blood like gravity.
He says the half-moon cut is fate marking him.

With my father I am still a child.
Looking at this, my own moon tonight,
It regards me with its huge, inscrutable, camel's eye.
Knowing all the answers, unavailing, mute.

Michael Kirkham

Night Thoughts

Abruption: a sudden silence between us.
Back to back, facing away,
walling out we are walled in
infinitely apart, space pouring
into us, a vast absence into us:
cast off adrift in the feral night.
Outside is inside: we are spilled out
usurped: the constant grind and groan
of the city swelling the silence. A word
has done this. Which a word must undo.

Michael Hamburger

Towards Equanimity

Brightest July between the darkenings
But cold, as though a waiting now for autumn,
Winter again, perhaps another spring
Of jonquils drenched, plum blossom perishing,
Ripped by the winds at war.

If light behind the eyes
Refuses eager reciprocity
Dimmer it was before,
Blacked out against the bombers,
So spared the recognition
By searchlight of their mission
To set ablaze or, blasting, raze the house.

Seeing, from first to last
Is a response to the sun,
Sun's moon at leat, far glitter
From some more alien planet.
No war was total, no window wholly blind
While one night's candle guttered.

The stored light, memory's,
Can that sustain a seeing?
A film's, it flashes by
Faster than breath, than any creature's being,
Human or butterfly.

Here, our survival's house,
Rot grows preposterous.
Outside, wronged nature breeds
Thicker and denser weeds,
In limbs a weariness, cross-fire of pain
Leave late exertions vain –

To antiquated lovers, you had me
Through clash and crash and clutter
Still, too, the morning sky,
Earthlight of evening primrose opening,
At night cow's moan, owl's cry,
Homed? heard? remembered? hints of house martins' mutter.

Timor mortis? Too well
I have rehearsed the going,
Before the bombs fell learned
That loss of love not life was their undoing
Who young were numbed, conscripted to the hell
That turns to dusk each dawn –

Yet need not, did not when
Half-blinded we faced fire,
By rote, by regimen,
Behind blank eyes for fire's sake, for the sun's
Though that fire could go out, all light withdrawn.

Recurrence even calls
For change behind the eyes;
From births and burials
A blur of strangeness clings
To long familiar places, features, things.
Dredged up with flux deposits, they surprise.
Re-hung, this drawing of you girlish gathers
Meaning from all you've been.

Lingering now, we're blessed
With slowness, let eyes rest
On continuities,
Darknesses, lights that mingle and seem one,
So many we have seen.

Jay Parini

Borges in Scotland

In the dismal garden at Pilmour
I watched old Borges, blind man leaning
on his stick among the iron trunks of beech,
a wing-dark canopy of claws above him.

Gusts of salt wind swayed the trees,
rippling the feathers of the bracken floor.
'It's rooks,' he said, ears opening like palms.
The empty headlights of his eyes turned up.

So Borges listened and was birds.
A soot-cloud rose, world-blackening,
the hard-by thunder of a thousand birds
who called his name now: Borges, Borges.

Peter Dale

Kids' Game

That whizz of a kids' game,
he on the lines, joins, cracks
in the roadway's concrete slabs:

to foot-tag the shadow
of runners on those lines,
lank shanks in the fading light.

One summer time.
But still the names come back
to the last man ...

Catch as catch can
and close on one of the missed
to sign off on this

Heugh

For W.S. Milne

Ma luve it greits as deep an narra
    As cleaves the Linn o Dee
Whase skiran cletters in ma marra
    As na mair sall she.

Her bed is narra, na sae deep,
    The kirk athoot ae tree,
An there sae douce an saft her sleep
    She dreams na mair o me.

Wheesht, wheesht tha stushie, fa,
    Whilk blethers in ma lug.
I canna heark her laich laich ca –
    Her sough wadna lift a speug.

    Wheesht, wheesht tha haivers, fa,
        Tha slitteran in ma banes
    Canna mak ma sarra sma
        As tha may mirl thae stanes.

W S Milne

'Over you now the wild winds blow'

I have left my book for a while, my study,
for I thought I heard you singing an air
in that hour when you liked repose,

when, with a light hand, you picked a rose
(all was ablaze, I lived in your smile,
and there was no shadow there).

Gone by the innumerable years!
Little did we know the ways we would travel,
my dove, my beautiful one!

All is now laden with tears.
Time has mocked our lives
                              gently, sweetly,
and you live, past all clamour now.

Harry Guest

Florum Imagines

I

VIOLETS

Their colour draws darkness
from the wrong side of the soil.

They give the daytime back as night –
sparks from those grief-lamps
hung on ceilings of the silent kingdom
in lieu of stars.

They hint at an afterworld
shining with mourning –
at moments draped in shadow
                       in sorrow
and summers muffled
beyond the reach of light
                       of normal light.

II

DANDELION

Yellow, it follows
the sun to the west

In autumn grey stars
fixed to thin needles
form a sphere of seeds
counting the hour
when children make time
drift over grass

A bald pitted head
all that is left
once time has been told

III

SPEEDWELLS

A healing farness
encourages our gaze
beyond the milestones set by the spring
displaying evidence
of a spaciousness hard to credit
beneath the autocracy of low noons.

Now unconfined,
February's tyrant gone,
we walk still barely able to trust
this newfound species of freedom.

Insignificant holes
punched in the green laneside
let in the first
immensity of light.

Sam Gardiner

Nursery Walks

No cemetery walks on Tuesdays,
when he descends from his 9th floor flat
and visits both garden centres
on the No 51 bus route.

The bus kneels down when it notes
his walking stick, and shivers
while he climbs aboard, placing his feet
too carefully for safety,

in travesty of when he chained
the swaying crowns on felling days.
Young trees, seedlings to saplings,
pine and oak, beech and birch,

bring him their distinct scents on the fire,
their aromatic ringlets from the plane,
and when grown tall and ready for the axe
their different voices in the wind.

Ian Caws

Requiem for a Downland Shepherd

There were stars, tossed in dim blankets, and tunes
heard from his whistle when lambing was done;
there was night on the downs, sounds of sheep bells,
    then, particular dawns
    at the worst time of year when squalls
re-entered his mind like a distant train.

These things reminded him it was the storm
he feared as rain rolled down the linseed oil
in his clothing or his vast umbrella.
    By his stove he felt warm
    as shadows changed shape and colour
flicked on the costrel where he kept his ale.

Rain, when he pushed the door, would not let up
and he noticed an old bilbo angled
in the ground, wattle hurdles, stacked and dark.
    These things he knew would keep
    like his flat back Southdowns, the flock
he loved best, their wool so fine and tangled.

He was old now, had become one weather,
his crook and lantern not far from his bed
in the brown, wheeled hut. But just this last time
    he let the hours gather
    until they took shape beside him,
a life, a death, and words that stayed unsaid.

André Frénaud

I Have Never Forgotten You

Nameless now and faceless
Nothing of your gaze or pallor

Freed from the assault of my desire
                Upon your capricious image
Stripped of the false confession of time
Ransomed by the false coin of love,
All such gains lost –
Free of you now
Free as a dead one
Living alone the seamy life
Dallying with stones and leaves

Though I slip between breasts of bitches
I still lie in your absence,
On the living corpse you make
Through your power to overcome me
Even to the end of my silence.

Translated from the French by **William Oxley**

Ángelos Sikelianós

(Sikelianós, 1884-1951, was the last great traditional poet of Greece, 'a giant who encompassed and possessed all of Hellenism's spiritual legacy'. Some of his greatest poems were written against the Occupation.)

Acrocorinth

Sunset on Acrocorinth fired
The rock all ruddy. From the waves
Came a sweet smell of seaweed-leaves,
Driving my lissom stallion wild.

Foam on the bit; his white of eye
Was fully bared. He champs, and strains
To loose my fist that grips the reins,
And into open space leap free.

Was it the hour? The teeming smells?
The deep salt of the *pélagos*?
The distant breathing of the wood?

Ah! had *meltémi* but endured
A little longer, I had held
The reins and flanks of Pegasus!

Meltémi: a seasonal rough sea-wind. *Pélagos*: open sea.

Translated by **Timothy Adès**

Doric

Shorn at the nape her tresses,
like Dorian Apollo;
she lay, like ice, in vapours
dense as her bed was narrow.

You shot her full of arrows,
Artemis! Still a virgin,
cold honeycomb of members
she locks, constricting passion.

Sleeked for the ring his muscles;
upon the lass he places
his knee, as one who wrestles.

He breaks her two hands' buttress;
slow, with one cry, they mingle
their lips, their sweats' embraces!

Translated by **Timothy Adès**

The Garden At Mistrá

Ta-ýgetos! From peaks that gleam all icy with a silver beam,
Amid the breeze that ever blows both sure and soft from melting snows,
In downy golden years of youth, in dawn's bright flash of flame,
The heavenly twins' white horses and their matchless chariot came;
Set low between her brothers both a-tiptoe on the beam,
In gown immortal, flowing down, like water, Helen came!

In the rosy light of dawn for You, my great-eyed holy Lady,
all the ding-dong bells were ringing, from Mistrá to Kalamáta.

O may my hand in prayer grasp the flower of the rose:
like a dove the passing hour on a sure wing goes.

On the high-arched windows the holy hour that passes
is a virgin lamp all shining before the iconostases.

Slim pillars on light arches, you are like the cyparisses
that soar up over waterfalls, on rocky precipices.

Garden of archangels where the wind-hovers play,
whose wing-beats fan the painted saints that fade and pass away!

There's a bee moaning loud from the old bell-tower,
for the mother of the hive, and the bell's a pendant flower.

Sword of Mount Ta-ýgetos, so quick to snuff the sun,
your draughts of shade refresh us as your temple-vaults have done.

O I dreamed amid the lilies and the garden-plants
that You, the Queen of All, danced a doe's merry dance.

Angels frisked around You, as I paid your Grace obeisance:
was it Eros blew me forward? I was saying my Eleïsons.

They crossed their wings so quick (I heard the rustle, do not doubt)
and raised them to the middle, with a turn-and-turn-about.

Your garden's bright with rose-beds, apple-trees and cherries,
almonds in abundance, and bunches of berries.

Greet me as you greet the little bird that comes along,
singing in the blessed shade its own sweet song.

I would not taste of all the fruit, but the ripest and the best:
ready and about to fall, by the birds caressed.

I'll water all your flower-beds, stooping to the splash,
just as does the blackbird, to give my face a wash.

My Lady, I shall rest beneath your white grape-vines,
in the bower where your crowding camomile twines.

Garden of archangels where the wind-hovers play,
refreshing all the painted saints that fade and pass away!

Translated by **Timothy Adès**

Mount Ta-ýgetos looms over the ruins of Mistrá and Sparta. Helen, not yet 'of Troy', was a pure and semi-divine bride.
Sikelianós titled this poem 'From the Prologue to Plethon'. Plethon of Mistrá, a leader of the Greek and Italian Renaissance, attended the Council of Florence, 1439, firing Cosimo de' Medici with enthusiasm for Plato.

© *With acknowledgements to Mr Costas Bournazakis.*

Güven Turan

Poem to Snow on the Way

I don't like the sky's whiteness.
Snow must surely fall
On the heels of this perpetual rain.
Snow from mountains lopped of trees,
Bringing depression and lethargy,
Like morning drowsiness descending
On indolent divans and balconies.
Snow which will mask
Thickets and thorns
Stained by the hunters with blood,
Will erase the tracks of death
And donate new killings:
A frozen goldfinch, a nightjar.
Feathers will multiply in the bridal beds.

A carniverous animal. It smells the air. A rusty smell that licks and scorches the nostrils. The air I breathe is damp and makes us shiver. It smells of snow. It buries its nose in its armpits. In the season of following tracks and of warm steaming blood, it stretches and makes the hair on the back of the neck stand on end.

Screams all night.
The northern blast moaned like animals in pain.
In trackless fields
Where mud no longer bubbles,
They set traps for bold sparrows;
With the same old scarecrows.
Now is the time to produce the well-oiled guns
From their fading cases of dried-up skins.

The porous firewood smokes and sizzles with damp. Echoes of rain. In the metal pipe. The room rings with sound like days when endless herds pass by. Now night is for love-making.

Tomorrow the pheasants retreat;
The crested birds arrive, the mallard ducks,
The tiny fieldfare: under the leafless poplars

And oaks the hunters lie in wait;
Green laurels half-open.
We continue the chase
Without end.

Now the mountains are tired. The mist comes down to linger for days and can't be shaken off. Rain rends the clifftops. Frost works its way into the deepest cracks. The first snow whirls into the heart of the valley, and in secluded places silence spreads further than autumn's uproar.

November 1968, Samsun.

Translated from the Turkish by **Ruth Christie**

W. S. Milne

The Poetry of Nessie Dunsmuir

It is a pity that Nessie Dunsmuir's poetry has been overshadowed by that of her more famous husband, the Scottish poet W. S. Graham. In a recent issue of the poetry magazine, *PN Review*, for example, she is interviewed about her husband's life and work with no mention at all made of her own poetry. Again, this is a pity for although her poetic output is small, it has considerable artistic merit. The most significant of her publications is *Ten Poems* which was re-published (after a forty year gap) in 1988 as a handsome pamphlet by Anthony Astbury's Greville Press in Warwick. There is a whole imaginative realm encompassed in the deceptively small space of these ten lyric poems, and I wish to concentrate on these as I believe they cohere as a group with intertwined themes and passions.

Dunsmuir is a poet with a precise sense of craft, and a loving, embracing rhythm. Poetry for her is 'this wordy ferment in the fingers,' 'this sailing hunger capsized in the breast,' the writer's 'quick hand' reacting to the mind's passion and intellect (what Bertrand Russell, in defining philosophy, called 'cold steel in a passionate hand'), 'the volcano's violence' of the two forces combined. A pre-eminent quality in Dunsmuir's poetry is that she is constantly looking for that which is miraculous and positive in life, something far removed from the depression and negativity prevalent in contemporary poetry. The future for her, for example, is betokened 'in tomorrow's flowering' (a lovely phrase I think) 'and summers all the wind with bees and rivers.' In transforming the plural noun 'summers' here into an active verb the poet is efforming intellect from matter, making an active principle out of brute inertia, pitching the grace of the spirit against the gravity of the physical world:

My breath is halted by origin's ape cry...

The sun goes down his golden length to lie
warm in my bone and in the warm earth's deep.
The night breaks in my heart. The berries gather
in a standing wheel of stars. The bright locks keep.

(from 'Acorn Mile Miracle Tree,' 1946)

The dates of the poems range from 1945 to 1949. They are not, however, set out chronologically which is interesting. She appears, on the contrary, to have set the poems out thematically, like a chain, for overall effect, the ten poems constituting, or forming, one inter-connected work or sequence. What we have here in this pamphlet is concentrated evidence of an intense five years of lyricism, a lyricism rooted in Dunsmuir's recurring obsession with love especially:

> I should have been more scrupulous
> of that first hour.
> More measured against future loss
> the live and lovely hazard where
> soul signalled soul
> through body's tenderness.
> But what had loss to do with us
> held there and holding all
> the blinding universe?
>
>   (from 'For A Winter Lover,' 1948)

Strangely perhaps, given the content of this poem, what first strikes one on reading Dunsmuir's poetry is a love of domestic comfort (an environment, let's admit it, not much hymned in recent decades), what she calls 'the breathing hearth,' a home 'roofed with rose of fire' (see below), a relishing of domestic security, 'housed in the halls' where 'the bright locks keep,' as she phrases it in 'Acorn Mile Miracle Tree.' The quotidian round of a household life is cherished, but not without intelligent doubt and uncertainty. Habit, routine, custom (as Proust has taught us) is both a creator and a destroyer, a creator of comfort, yes, maybe, but also a destroyer of creativity. Just such a conflict, psychological and urgent, is evident throughout this collection of poems, as in the first of them, 'I Would Have Chosen Children' (1946):

> I would have chosen children,
> the breathing hearth. And made my own
> ritual in winter, birth and bone.
> Not this wordy ferment in the fingers,
> this sailing hunger capsized in the breast.
> I would have chosen children,
> and roofed with rose of fire their early east.

We have to wait until the nineteen-sixties, for the work of Sylvia Plath, to hear this plangent female note in poetry again, a note of 'homely' angst redolent of Emily Brontë and Emily Dickinson. In terms of her own female contemporaries, I think Dunsmuir's poetry stands up with the best of Laura Riding, Kathleen Raine, and Anne Ridler; the clearest influence upon her work, however, perhaps not unsurprisingly, is that of her husband, sharing as she does some of his themes and obsessions. There is, for example, in Dunsmuir's poems an autobiographical landscape similar to that proletarian one found in W. S. Graham's poems, 'The Children of Greenock,' 'The Children of Lanarkshire,' 'the loud Clydeside' of 'The White Threshold', and 'Greenock At Night I Find You,' for example.

Dunsmuir gives us three or four of the finest poems I know of on the topic of mining, especially of coal-pits and their machinery, as good as anything in Jack Clemo for instance. These mining poems possess an authentic, lived experience (unlike some of those pseudo working-class poems one associates with the 'thirties, for example) like Graham's own, or that of their fellow Clydesider, Eddie Linden.

We have here a vista of 'galleries' (of coal that is, not art, the ambiguity of the phrase being quite deliberate on Dunsmuir's part, separating the two, very diverse social milieux), of 'pit-wheels,' 'the descending cage,' the 'nightshift,' and the 'dayshift,' 'the black underground,' 'the coalface,' 'the pit-head,' and the sun's 'blinding shaft':

> Behind my head the falling sun
> reddens the rim of the pit's dark wheels.
> The night-wind rising in sadness stills
> the children's late cries from the green.
> The dark falls down. The cables whine.
>
> I walk beside my younger brother
> past the fire-doors towards the edge
> where men wait ready for the cage.
> In the darkness dropping its silent name
> my fear falls past the night-startled men.
>
> The children play by the whirring wheels.
> Up happy years their glances drift.
> Do games grow to that waiting shaft
> and make belief those galleries shine?
> The cage falls like a guillotine.
>
> ('Stanis Pit,' 1947)

Dunsmuir's poetry then is very personal, rooted as it is in a real community, unusual in modern poetry, reminding one of the early work of D. H. Lawrence, and prefiguring the realism of Philip Larkin. 'The fiery slag,' 'the winding gear,' 'the cooling tower,' are all familiar images, or symbols, to Dunsmuir in her intimate industrial landscape:

> The cage lit by men's faces
> winds down the shining voices
> to the black galleries of coal.
> If only their youth would leave him unscathed,
> the night-walking men taken into the dark.

(from 'The Night-Walking Men Taken Into The Dark,' 1949)

(Notice how consciously that last phrase, 'the night-walking men', echoes the earlier 'night-startled men' of 'Stanis Pit,' establishing links across the sequence.) Even seemingly neutral phrases such as 'the light unwinding' from the penultimate stanza of 'The Night-Walking Men Taken Into The Dark' carry within them the seed of that industrial landscape, hints and intimations of it, reminding one of the chiaroscuro etchings of Henry Moore or Norman Cornish.

In 'Raith Pit' (1947) the poet asks:

> What recompense in what strange coinage
> held you in noisy dust of the descending cage
> hooded within the coalface rumble
> hearing your summer wear away?

The poet expects no reply, for the radicalism is a 'given' element, tacit, assumed, accepted; the tone is rhetorical, quietly reflecting this life led in the dark, evincing at one and the same time a patient strength and a 'furious love' not always found in poems that tend towards the political. The conflict, as in all good literature, is not resolved (as it might be in the political realm, for instance), but is left open to all the tragic winds of life. As for Nessie Dunsmuir's working-class background, we see it again reflected, or refracted rather, in the poetry of her husband. By 1949 we find W S Graham writing of 'Nessie' in the poem 'The White Threshold,' for example (from the book of that title):

> And as a child on Dechmont side
> She looked down her loud seasons
> Down on pits and wheels
> Unwinding in diving cages
> Young kings mad under meadows...

> A woman folkhomed by red Lanarkshire's slag
> Held in foster heart
> She endured the furnace in the sky.

Some of the phrases to be found in Dunsmuir's poetry are akin to those found in Graham's, who writes of the 'hammer yards' of Clydeside, 'the furnaced city' of his childhood, the neighbouring 'rivetting yards,' 'bone-works,' 'the welding lights in the shipyards' which 'flower blue,' suggesting that both poets may have received inspiration and support from each other, working mutually, much like that other Scottish literary couple, Edwin and Willa Muir, when they translated the novels of Franz Kafka into English.

Besides this industrial inheritance, Dunsmuir's poetry also educes a pastoral landscape full of spiritual conviction bordering on the biblical at times:

> Here by the window blackthorn and elder tree
> sharpen my sight to love...
>
> Here by my head blackbird and beaded tree
> borrow me back from Easter's cross and kiss.
> Bracken fronds hand me light.
> My own beginning eyes
> load at the sill the buds breaking to white.
>
> (from 'By The Window,' 1945)

The spiritual landscape of these poems is not that of strict Christian doctrine or dogma, however, but rather one of wide Christian reading and a sense of Christian cultural tradition, pressing upon the concerns of our more everyday language:

> The Easter fields of children turn again
> the legend's wheel. The painted eggs begin
> to roll our death away.
> In the cold April day
> each child is blessed and lies with Spring within.
>
> (from 'By The Window,' again)

Or this, once more from 'For A Winter Lover':

> Stranger in my arms
> man clown and angel
> bearing like flowers
> the everlasting annunciation.

The overall effect of these poems is that of a coalescing of secular language with the divine, as in the love poems of John Donne, for carnal ends:

> My harlot self in crimsons
> blesses where summer shines
> his name upon the stones.
>
> In the blaze of my veins' history
> his law-breaking mercury
> changes each voice I carry.
>
> All thoughts are passport to his quiet room.
> My searching joy without least let or hindrance
> brings back imagined news from his last glance.
> His breath my life, my death were his indifference.
>
>   (from 'He For Whose Sake,' 1947)

The achieved tone, as in other modern female poets like Marianne Moore and Elizabeth Bishop (or more recently, perhaps, in the work of poets like Fleur Adcock and Louise Glück) is one of doubt, of agnosticism, but one which still carries after-echoes, or after-images, of faith. In Dunsmuir's poetry, 'falls,' or 'fall' is a key-word (in 'To My Father' she says we 'fall to words,' suggesting a loss of grace and innocence). We have already seen how 'The cage falls like a guillotine' in 'Stanis Pit'; in the same poem we find also 'the falling sun,' and 'my fear falls'; in 'The White Word' we find 'I listen and the star falls,' phrases which sit synergetically with the miner's 'cage' (representing spiritual captivity, as much as wage-labour I feel) and 'the waiting shaft' of the mine.

If this language, or imagery, instantiates a sense of our fallen state (what Simone Weil calls our 'gravity,' our boundedness to earth — very literally so in the case of Dunsmuir's coalface workers), 'gravity calling all falling wonders home' Dunsmuir calls it in 'Acorn Mile Miracle Tree,' then our ascent from this condition is also hinted at in our Christian dispensation, intimated here in the 'word's orchard' (The Garden of Eden), Leviathan, the 'olive branch and burning bush,' and Christ's parable of the mustard seed:

> Set your word's orchard fair to find my ear.
> Your tongue has olive branch and burning bush.
> O over me can fall the fabulous peace
> or scorch of glory sponsor my release.
>
> I listen and the star falls. The white bird
> starts up from your breath. And for this space
> whale and Orion, earthquake and mustard seed
> merge.
>
> (from 'The White Word,' 1949)

Or this, again from 'He For Whose Sake':

> He for whose sake this ambiguity
> leads me by wilderness and careless waters
> towards my dear resurrection, still maintains
> forever my watching breath stilled for his coming

– the second line here reflecting the metre and the language of The Psalms I feel, and the references to 'wilderness,' 'ressurection,' and 'his coming,' clear enough.

Interestingly, the 'voice' here is very similar to that tone we find in Graham's own love poem to Nessie of 1970, 'I Leave This At Your Ear,' (subtitled *For Nessie Dunsmuir*, in fact):

> I leave this at your ear for when you wake,
> A creature in its abstract cage asleep.
> Your dreams blindfold you by the light they make.
>
> The owl called from the naked-woman tree
> As I came down by the Kyle farm to hear
> Your house silent by the speaking sea.
>
> I have come late but I have come before
> Later with slaked steps from stone to stone
> To hope to find you listening for the door.
>
> I stand in the ticking room. My dear, I take
> A moth kiss from your breath. The shore gulls cry.
> I leave this at your ear for when you wake.

Once again, one feels that there are synergies at work here between the two poetries of wife and husband, a shared symbolism (of 'the cage' for instance – one thinks also, for example, of Graham's first book of poems entitled *Cage Without Grievance*, of 1942) and a shared concern of waiting and watching for love. (It is possible that Graham himself, on the evidence of his own poems, may have learned a thing or two about craft and phrase-making from his wife or, at any rate, there was a reciprocal process at work between them.) A similar preoccupation is present in Graham's poem from 1949, 'Listen. Put On Morning' (in his third book of poems, *The White Threshold* – notice again the homely title):

> Listen. Put on morning.
> Waken into falling light.

Both poets' work evince what Graham calls the 'kindling power' of poetry, its light and revelation, especially as manifested in the radiance of love; 'my eyes inherit,' Dunsmuir says, 'a lightstruck world' (in 'For A Winter Lover'). Here, in the small compass of this pamphlet, we have poems written 'from the deep heart' (see Graham's poem, 'The White Threshold'), strong passions focused in 'the lens of language' (see his poem, 'The Don Brown Route,' in *Malcolm Mooney's Land*, 1970), like 'the little village/Of a new language' of her husband's poem 'The Lying Dear' of 1970.

Sometimes in the pamphlet (it is only very rarely though, it must be said) one hears the voices of *The New Apocalypse* anthology of 1940, those of G. S. Fraser and Vernon Watkins for example, as well as the likes of George Barker, David Gascoyne and Dylan Thomas, breaking through in obscure, refractory, hieratic phrasing (as in 'In my blood's roadway,' for instance, or 'The apparatus of the Spring,' or 'the algebra of ocean,' or 'the daystrong sun'), but these are over-ridden by Dunsmuir's novel and original apprehensions and apperceptions. She never really requires such second-hand clothes. Her voice is unique and confident enough without such borrowings.

The 'lyrical action' (the phrase is Graham's own) of Dunsmuir's poetry is as clear as a bell for any reader alert and intelligent enough to follow the nuances of her work:

> Into the morning wind
> the pit-wheels whirr and grind
> from the black underground
> its nightshift boys and men,
> and my father one.

> Light stands, pearl in his eyes.
> Now, twice released, he sees
> the long coasts of the skies
> sail their bright dayshift down
> the blinding shaft of the sun.
>   (from 'Raith Pit')

This is poetry of the highest order, embodying Kathleen Raine's 'the holy fire of passion' wherein, joyously, 'hope's waters rise and play' (see her poems 'Passion,' and 'The Spring').

Dunsmuir, like all good poets, has the ability to find the exact word or phrase to suit the emotion, and the vision, perhaps more importantly, to grasp life's grace each day anew. Her poetry redeems what Roland John has called 'the sullen world.' In her poetry, thoughts are 'enchanted into form' (a phrase from Graham's 1945 poem 'The Narrator,' published in 2ND *Poems*). And it is to W. S. Graham's own poetry that we turn again for some final, loving glimpses of his wife. First of all we see him writing of her generously, richly, counterpoising 'the mill' of his 'pinched words' (pinched from her possibly?) with her own art of writing, 'that has a mouth of flowers to the naked grave,' contemplating her weeding the garden in 'Except Nessie Dunsmuir,' a poem from 1945:

> For she grew richly up singing weedwater high
> As wallflowers round her shy child her fairest
> April and prodigal tongue that looped in a spray
> Wades the three wounds from Calder's precious home...
>
> Except my tongue dipped in the weeding girl
> Except her arrival over the sour grass blessed
> With the red word out of her cried-out enemies.
> And she by the beggar of a common sake
> Speaks through her licking joy with a drop of grief.

The second quotation is from her husband's final poem in his *Collected Poems 1942–1977* (Faber Paperbacks, 1979), 'To My Wife at Midnight,' a loving, last, dedicatory poem:

> Nessie, don't let my soul
> Skip and miss a beat
> And cause me to fall...

> Nessie Dunsmuir...
> Are you to say goodnight
> And kiss me and fasten
> My drowsy armour tight?
>
> My dear camp-follower,
> Hap the blanket round me
> And tuck in a flower.

'What is the language using us for?' Graham asks at one point in his work, and his wife's sequence replies eloquently, *to write poetry of a high order*.

The final quotation is from Dunsmuir's poem 'To My Father,' a quietly touching elegy which epitomises the 'furious love' in her work allied to the 'cold eye' of the artist:

> In loneliness your waking hand from rest
> broke bread with morning. Inside your sleeping heart
> can bud no beat of comfort from a daughter's hurt,
> or waters of myrrh to rise and call you blessed.
> Lie then at home where coal hills heap in fire
> and keep you their bright company in your shared shire.

As William Empson said, the critic can never exhaust the poetry (if it is any good, that is) she or he is writing about. Readers must find the richness for themselves. There is more than enough of such richness in Nessie Dunsmuir's poetry, a rich vein of ore for the reader to mine for sure.

Greg Delanty

The New Voyager

To Daniel, as I recall your mother having her monitor check during the 2000 Presidential election and the monitor picking up a local radio.

It was uncanny that morning how the Doppler,
    flying-saucered across the globe of your mother,
picked up our future commander-in-chief promising a golden world,
    his voice coming through like a scratched record – you curled
        in your womb-whirligig, our terrestrial.
Shades of Voyager's gold-coated record to be played by extraterrestrials
    light years away, spinning with the world's salutary
        lingoes, music, flora and fauna – many already history –
without mention of war-making; the needless extra terrestrial
    lacrimae rerum; or the excluded photograph of a couple
        strolling naked, the woman expecting,
vetoed not because they're the spitting image of the starving
    myriads (each belly-bloated with nothing),
        but in blushing shame of the body.
Now that you've disembarked your mum module,
    I launch, not without apology,
        this ephemerally sealed capsule.

Daniel Tobin

World Music

Greg Delanty, *Collected Poems 1986–2006*, Carcanet, £14.95.

The growth of a poet's mind, to borrow Wordsworth's well-trodden phrase, can be followed in part by the distance covered from the first place to the wider arenas of experience beyond the poet's original world. That journey may be solely a matter of the quality of consciousness, like Emily Dickinson or R.S. Thomas, or it may be literally as well as consciously enacted. One thinks of Wordsworth himself, and Bishop and Walcott. Either way the poet's work has to evolve artistically, has to carry those first inklings of poetry from what was initially seen and felt to what was unforeseen and unexpected, and it must do so by continually drawing the line between them and further out again. Greg Delanty is the second kind of poet, a poet for whom the *errancy* of the journey is a spur to the artist's vital perspective not only on where he comes from but where he proposes to go.

Few poets of Delanty's age – he just turned forty-eight – have the benefit of a retrospective volume covering the breadth of the career thus far, though in the case of Delanty's poetry, Carcanet's decision to publish such a volume affords readers the opportunity to survey his substantial body of work. (Paul Muldoon is another, though a collected volume for a poet so young is virtually unheard of in the United States, which might suggest a substantial difference between the reception and publication of poetry on the American side of the Atlantic, and Delanty's work inhabits both worlds). That body of work is shaped largely by the poet's emigration in the 1980s from his home in Cork, Ireland, to America and eventually to Vermont where he now resides and teaches. One of the so-called 'New Irish' who left Ireland for the United States before the arrival of 'the Celtic Tiger,' Delanty's work speaks not only to the long history of Irish emigration and the experience of being a contemporary Irish immigrant in America, but also out of a desire to make his own journey emblematic for his time. The fundamental tension that spurs Delanty's poetry crosses the domestic with the wayward, the retrospective with the prospective, and the result is a body of work that has grown steadily from book to book in depth, invention, and ambition.

The generative tension between the poet's domestic inclinations and the spur of departure manifests itself throughout the poems of his first two books, *Cast in the Fire* (1986) and *Southward* (1992), which are combined in the present volume. The felt attentions of these early poems turn to family, young love, home, place, and gradually open onto travel and the emigrant's life abroad in America; naturally what follows are the considerations that the move forces on his relationship to home. Appropriately, Delanty's first book was published in Ireland with Dolmen Press and his second in the United States with Louisiana State University Press—he is a poet of those two worlds from early on. There are echoes of Kavanagh in these early poems, as in the last line of 'Leavetaking' where the departing emigrant and his father wave 'eternally to each other,' recalling the older poet's 'In Memory of My Mother,' though Delanty's more traditionally formal inclinations are also tested by the influence of American free verse, as in 'Epistle from a Room in Winston-Salem, North Carolina' and 'The Loudest Sound.' The draw and celebration of domestic life is strong here, and remains consistently so in Delanty's work, but also strong is the 'outering' current surfacing from under, as in 'Nightmare,' one of the very best of the early poems:

> Though it has never happened, you know
> How it feels to fall overboard at night;
> To discover your cries go unheard by the crew,
> Drowned out by the wind, sea and boat.

Delanty's deft management of this sonnet with its off-rhymes showcases his ability to work conversationally inside a demanding form, a facility owed in part to Heaney as well as to Kavanagh, though beyond its formal achievement the poem succeeds in transforming the nightmare description into metaphor: 'It is not water you tread, but darkness. / The dreaded creatures baiting you are in you.' The poem is suggestive of the trajectory of Delanty's subsequent work – an outward journey that mirrors the inward journey of the poet negotiating personal, political, artistic, and spiritual allegiances – as are other poems such as 'The Master Printer' and 'Home From Home.'

If Delanty's first two books introduce a young poet who practises his craft with laudable facility and distinction, then the books that follow showcase a poet deepening into maturity and coming into his own with a distinctive voice. *American Wake* (1995) includes many fine poems that explore the poet as both emigrant and immigrant and yet somehow never wholly one or the other. Here is the beginning of 'The Fifth Province':

> Meeting in a café, we shun the cliché of a pub.
>   Your sometime Jackeen accent is decaffed
> like our coffee, insisting you're still a Dub.
>   You kid about being half & halfed.

The insecurity of being, proverbially, neither one thing nor the other is admirably evoked by Delanty's precise depiction of the American scene, which is counterpointed by his use of Irish diction –'Jackeen' and 'Dub'– and further heightened by the witty repartee about being 'half & halfed.' As the stanza continues the confusion of identity turns inward –'the people populating your dreams now are / American,' the poet observes, though they are back home in Ireland. In the stanzas that follow the poem pursues its exploration of the emigrant's ambiguous sense of identity by moving us from dreamscape to legend – Brendan's voyage and Hy-Brasil – to history without leaving the café, and it does so believably, without forcing its conceit, because of the confidence and ease of Delanty's voice. It is no small achievement to be able to carry off a poem of seeming immediacy without disrupting what John Gardner in another context called 'the continuous fictional dream,' the sense of inhabiting the world created by the writer. So much of contemporary poetry wants to dazzle on the page, as if the poet really had very little confidence in what was being written – written and not said. The result is often cacophony or melodrama. Delanty's poems invariably speak to the reader; they invite the reader into the scene, and upon re-reading the poems reveal the nuances of their artistry. 'The Heritage Center, Cobh, 1993,' 'America,' 'On the Renovation of Ellis Island' and many other poems in *American Wake* evince this quality, Delanty's conversational voice on the page folding together serious emotional content, intellectual ideas, politics, historical and literary allusions, and dramatic scene, very often with a comedic riff. One senses that, for Delanty, comedy is how he keeps the darkness which surfaces in the early poem 'Nightmare' at bay, but it never devolves into slapstick or vacuous irony as it does in many a lesser poet.

Tracing the arc of how the poems are arranged in *American Wake*, one sees that they are carefully placed to move from the emigrant's life in America, infused as it is in the poet's mind by history and legend, to the long poem 'The Splinters,' which is a tour-de-force suite for voices where figures from Irish literary history from Amergin to Louis MacNiece step up, as it were, to the camera to tell their tales. The book ends with 'The Children of Lir,' again an evocation from Irish legend and an analogy for 'all the exiles.' Delanty's next book, *The Hellbox* (1998), reverses course, moving as it does from poems about his father's life at the Eagle Printing Shop in Cork to the son's life as an emigrant in America, the land of the eagle. Many of the poems in this volume are not only moving elegies for a dead father, but performances on the page that use the lingo of the printer's art both to evoke the lost world of the father's trade but also to examine the nature of invention in the son's trade of poetry. The book to a poem is rife with invention, turning sonnets to new effect, and in one case – 'The Printer's Devil' – turning the print around entirely so one must read it upside down and backwards in a mirror. In effect what Delanty does in this poem, and in 'The Broken Type,' is make the physical poem on the page part of the performance actively as well as aurally. To fully get the poem you need to literally pick up the book. The American influence can be felt in *The Hellbox* in the poem 'We Will Not Play the Harp Backwards Now, No,' which answers Marianne Moore's 'Spenser's Ireland' by using the syllabic line adopted by that poem. An American cadence is also heard in the longer line employed in 'Striped Ink,' 'The Lost Way,' and in particular in the book's title poem where Irish diction and Cork slang mixes with an expansive structure running down the page, though it is always tuned to Delanty's ear which is never derivative of generic 'American' modes. That vocal admixture comes more and more to characterize his poems, and it speaks to the inclusive art he seeks to achieve. The poem 'The Hellbox' is an *ars poetica* in which the poet declares:

> All I want is not simply to parrot American voices,
>   reminding me of how the immigrants learned
> a new tongue, mimicking gramophone records
>   or following theatre stars from show to show,
> pronouncing actors lines, always a fraction behind,
>   till they knew every word...

Rather, Delanty spurs himself through multiple vocal exercises, from those as performative as the actors he invokes above, through a bit of self-conscious, self-mocking mimicry, to 'the cocky young cleric at St. Brendan's door, / refusing to leave till I've played the music of the world.' To be sure there is 'cockiness' in Delanty's poems, or more rightly an engaging confidence in the voice, though that voice is anything but stand-offish. It is inviting. The binding motif and ambition of Delanty's work is this desire to play the music of the world, both intimately in poems of domestic observance and more encompassingly in poems of searching migration.

In his two most recent collections, *The Blind Stitch* (2001) and *The Ship of Birth* (2003), Delanty's ambition to hold in a single thought the domestic and the errant in a manner broadly reminiscent of the physicist's desire to unify the quantum and galactic realms advances significantly beyond the imaginative poles of Ireland and America. There are poems in *The Blind Stitch* like 'The Speakeasy Oath,' 'The Memory Quilt,' and 'Tagging the Stealer' that explore what by now is Delanty's familiar territory of emigrant life and the relationship between his two homes, though these poems refuse to settle into complacent patterns. Each of these poems is an address – to the Irish poet-friend, to an American poet-friend, and to an American seamstress friend – in which the poet with characteristic verve and wit manages to portray human affection without affectation or sentimentality while at the same time articulating his art's ideals. 'Give us each just once / a poem equal to that unknown man's talking hand,' the poet muses watching the sign-language of the catcher to the pitcher during a baseball game – a kind of shibboleth for reading America as well as bringing its way with language into his art. The conceit that weaves the poems of *The Blind Stitch* together, however, begins with the thread that appears in the first poem, 'To My Mother, Eileen' and finishes with the final poem, 'The Blind Stitch,' a love poem for his wife. The book evolves between two movingly depicted domestic scenes, though what distinguishes this collection is Delanty's own passage to India in poems that add a still more worldly scope to the familiar pattern of this work. Not surprisingly, Delanty finds in India and Sri Lanka a kind of Asian objective correlative to Cork, though poems like 'The Emerald Isle, Sri Lanka' and 'Behold the Brahmany Kite' engage that world on its own terms from the poet's individual perspective – which is something one expects in a Delanty poem: the world embraced as given but reflected in the prism of the poet's idiosyncratic sight:

> And in my way I too believe in the kasti – the sacred
>   thread – of the elements
> stitching us all together...

What I have been calling Delanty's waywardness and errancy is not really the antithesis of his poetry's "homelier" impulses but it is, as it were, the flipside of the domestic coin, the yang to its yin. (Masculine and feminine poles also interplay in Delanty's work – his father is the presiding spirit of *The Hellbox*; his mother and his wife the presiding spirits of *The Blind Stitch.*) The title of *The Ship of Birth* embodies the idea of the errant, the wayward, the journey, but that journey arrives perforce in the domestic world, which is ultimately the world we all share in spite of the separate realms of our private lives. In this world where journeys and arrivals are at once miracles in themselves and harbingers of the wider realities, the birth of the poet's son bespeaks the emigrant nature of every life:

> I'm back again scrutinsing the Milky Way
>   of your ultrasound, scanning the dark
>   matter, the nothingness, that now the heads say
>   is chockablock with quarks and squarks,
> gravitons and gravatini, photons & photini....

If 'The Alien' joins together beautifully the seemingly contrasting impulses of Delanty's work then it also exemplifies one of the most appealing facets of this poet's voice – its welcoming quality that at the same time doesn't leave him at a loss for wit and imaginative play. At the same time, if *The Ship of Birth* suggests a book about miraculous arrivals, then it is also naturally a book of departures, for it also contains moving elegies for his mother. These elegies are continued in the section of new work, *Alcedama*, in which also appear a number of political poems about our disastrous treatment of the environment, among other brutal realities of our time. One such poem, 'US,' describes an apt analogy for large-scale American consumption in the burning of oil candles. There are quite a number of quietly (and overtly) political poems scattered through Delanty's work, like those in the pamphlet *Children of Chernobyl* (1996), also included in the volume. 'Aceldama' refers to the 'the field of blood' purchased by the priests and elders with Judas' thirty pieces of silver thrown down in the temple after he had betrayed Christ (Matthew 27: 5–8), and the poem of that title powerfully changes the context and resonance of the work that comes before:

> We drove down what seemed the curve
> of the earth, sandwiched in our Ford Anglia.
> We were happy as the colors of our beachball,
> a careless car full of mirth and singalong songs,
> songs that were mostly as sappy
> as the soppy tomato sandwiches sprinkled with sand,
> which is why they're called sandwiches our father said,
> sandwiched himself now in the ground between his mother
> and ours. What's the meaning of dead?

The poem's first sentence places us brilliantly at once in the domestic car and on the curve of the wider world and then moves us seamlessly line by line through the evocatively digressive thoughts of the poet recalling the scene. We come at once to be in the poet's mind and in the child's both arriving at the ultimate irrevocable question. From there the poem moves us more intimately inside the domestic bubble of the Delantys' Ford Anglia where the mother serves as a kind of guide to the children and now the recollecting poet as they survey a local hill field where the dead have been buried without recognition or headstone. She is an ordinary woman who has been transformed quietly by the poet into the family's Virgil, explaining the nature of this remote field that has become an image of the lost world, despite all its 'beautiful cities.' And what she awakens in the children, the poet, and the reader is not only the sense of human loneliness that 'shrouds' the family's 'bright time' and joins everyone together on the journey through birth and life into death, but the transfiguring presence of compassion. Such is the world Greg Delanty would have us encounter, and his music in this poem – the last in his *Collected* – achieves the measure of it. Delanty's is an important body of work for both sides of the Atlantic, and for English language poetry, and one can be sure that his vision will deepen and continue to grow only more encompassing.

Eavan Boland

Becoming the Hand of John Speed

How do you make a nation?
How do you make it answer to you?
How do you make its parts, its waterways
its wished-for blueness at the horizon point
take heed?

I have no answer. I was born in a nation
I had no part in making.

But sometimes late at night when I want to imagine
what it was to be a part of it
I take down my book and then I am

the agile mapping hand of John Speed
making *The Kingdome of Ireland, 1612*,

my pen moving over a swerve of contour,
my ink stroke adding an acre of ocean:

The Dublin hills surrender two dimensions.
Forests collapse, flattening all their wolves.

The Irish sea cedes its ancient tensions,
its gannets, gulls, cormorants all stopped
from flying away by their own silhouettes –

and you might say my nation has become
all but unrecognizable, but no

I remember the way it was when I was young,
wanting the place to know me at first glance
and it never did, it never did, and so

this is the way to have it, cut to size,
its waters burned in copper, its air unbreathed
its future neighbourhoods almost all unnamed –

and even the old, ocean-shaped horizon
surprised by its misshapen accuracy –

ready and flat and yearning to be claimed.

Tony Roberts

Eavan Boland, *New Collected Poems*, Carcanet, £14.95

What brings us back to some of our best poets is the simple fact that they write so well. Eavan Boland is one of them. In a celebrated career, she has pitted herself against the marginalisation of women, in poetry and in (Irish) historical life. If, in her explorations of womanhood, she has not as yet 'detonated' in the consciousness (to use her own image) to the degree that Plath, Rich and Bishop have, she has nevertheless produced a serious body of work, beautifully written. That is the achievement of *New Collected Poems*.

The earliest poems in this inclusive collection find her working solidly within the Irish tradition she has inherited, a tradition according to her memoir, *Object Lessons* (1995):

> which could never foresee her (a woman poet), but it is construed by men about men in ways which are poignant, compelling and exclusive.

The exclusiveness is, of course, the rub. Her earliest efforts are Yeatsian (the image of swans, the poet's craft). There are legends and myths, Irish political history, dedications to Mahon and Longley – to her it was a man's world, but not to everyone. Anne Stevenson, writing in the *PN Review*, took issue with Boland's claim 'to be disadvantaged by her national past'. She felt that Boland had not sufficiently sought out the poetry of women, being trapped between a pressure to embrace radical feminism and the desire to be accepted by her male peers.

However, in *Young Eavan and Early Boland*, Derek Mahon corroborates Boland's view. He writes that these were 'pre-feminist times' – implying her hand was forced – and adds sympathetically, 'Eavan wrote then, as she no longer does, for a notional *male* readership.'

Whatever tension this might have created for her privately, what one chiefly senses in these early poems, is a young poet brimming with enthusiasm and creativity. They are full of references to the arguments upon which life, poetry and thought are sustained in the young ('Belfast vs Dublin'). There are wry observations ('Requiem for a Personal Friend') and the clear hint of an ambiguous attitude to Yeats, whose impact is undeniable, but whose mind is 'stowaway', in 'Yeats in Civil War'. There is the highly accomplished Tennysonian echo, also, in 'The Winning of Etain'.

However, most interesting in light of Boland's later preoccupations, is three lines from 'From the Painting *Back from Market* by Chardin':

> I think of what great art removes:
> Hazard and death, the future and the past,
> This woman's secret history and her loves –

23 Poems (1962) and *New Territory* (1967) are accomplished early volumes, then, but Boland soon set a course to introduce to poetic art 'woman's secret history'.

The War Horse (1975) is a painful book. Its titles tell us so: 'A Soldier's Son', 'The Famine Road', 'Prisoners', 'The Hanging Judge'. In a time of violence, the poet's diction is combative, assailed. In the title poem, an escaped traveller's horse, returning to its field – now houses – disrupts the new order:

> He stumbles on like a rumour of war, huge,
> Threatening; neighbours use the subterfuge
>
> Of curtains; he stumbles down our short street
> Thankfully passing us. I pause, wait

The use of caesura and weighted syllables, the flimsy rationalisations and irony dramatise the futile evasions of 'a world betrayed'.

'The Famine Road' details the torture of the nineteenth century Irish poor, coerced into scraping roads to nowhere for the Relief Committee. It is a telling narrative, interspersed with the sufferers' consolations and the cold-blooded calculating words of the persecutors:

> Idle as trout in light Colonel Jones,
> these Irish, give them no coins at all; their bones
> need toil, their characters no less.

Even the love poems have an edgy feel about them. In 'The Other Woman', the poet balks against sharing her author husband with his heroines. In a more settled collection, the clever conceit of the poem would simply amuse. In the context of *The War Horse*, however, it alerts us to tension even within happiness.

Next came *In Her Own Image* (1980), an angry collection, firstly stripping the muse of her glamour and then stripping the line itself through subsequent poems, until what is left are versions of the maimed female self, defiant in the face of misogyny. 'In Her Own Image' and 'In His

Own Image' deal with the erasure of women's identity by violence and triviality. The book moves from pain to pain, with some ferocity. In 'Anorexic' the disgust, the impulse to self-destruct is captured in the image of the witch, the archetypal (male) image of ugliness and evil. 'Thin as a rib' she returns, ironically, to the comfort of man's side, denying the sensual life of 'sweat and fat and greed'. It is only in 'Menses' that the menstrual blood restores some self-image ('my light's my own').

Night Feed (1980) asserts, instead, the primacy of women's experience. Boland has worked through to a recognition of the new world of motherhood. It is not a woman's role, but her perspective that occupies the poet. Here she is immersed

> in the sort of light
> jugs and kettles
> grow important by
> ('Domestic Interior')

The book is not simply a celebration of the exhausting joys of motherhood. Other things prey – random thoughts, fears. Memories of a displaced childhood intrude in quiet moments. The daughter of an Irish diplomat and an artist mother, Boland spent some of her childhood, unhappy, in London. In 'Lights' there is a memory dream of a return to Ireland on board ship, which ends uneasily with, 'And all the lights I love/ leave me in the dark.'

For all that, *Night Feed* has more recourse to love and family than earlier collections. In terms of Eavan Boland's direction, a key poem is 'The Muse Mother', where the poet yearns to learn her neighbour's 'language': the history of Irish women. Boland's search is always for her own Irish identity. Again the short lines with their three stressed syllables carry the zeal:

> able to sing the past
> in pure syllables,
> limning hymns sung
> to belly wheat or a woman -
>
> able to speak at last
> my mother tongue.

Her next book, *The Journey* (1987), deploys 'the brisk herbs of language' ('The Oral Tradition') to telling effect, but the journey itself is a dark one, into memory, into suffering. It opens with 'I Remember', the poet as an inquisitive nine year old evidently living in some London luxury:

> the room had been shocked into a glacier
> of cotton sheets thrown over the almond
> and vanilla silk of the French Empire chairs.

It is to such descriptive touches as this, that William Logan was referring when he dubbed the poet 'the bard of fabric' in a *New York Times* review, which saw her work as 'transformed only by a love of pure detail, of the incandescence of the visual'. Such criticism, however, suggests indifference both to the poetry's sensuousness and to the quiet, cumulative creation of imagery.

The contrast in this poem is with 'bombed-out, post war London', and the girl is as unhappy as she is privileged. Possibly she senses what other immigrants are oblivious to: that a new language will eventually bring only a 'passable imitation/ of what went before' ('Mise Eire').

In 'Self-Portrait on a Summer Evening' Boland considers Chardin's painting of a woman. This artist and the poet are in frequent sympathy, since he chose to depict the beauty in reality:

> I am Chardin's woman
>
> edged in reflected light,
> hardened by
> the need to be ordinary.

'Ordinary' is always an honourable adjective in the poet's hands.

'The Oral Tradition' celebrates truth and resonance, but tradition is something Boland, the exile, experiences – as it were – through glass. Her substantial imaginative and lyrical gifts bring her close to past experiences, but never close enough. In 'Fever' she writes of her grandmother, dead in a fever ward, of 'the histories I never learned/ to predict the lyric of', and experience that 'cannot be/shaken out from words or beaten out/ from meaning.'

Her association with her suffering womanhood is the thread in *The Journey*. In the substantial title poem, Sappho takes the poet on a Virgilian journey into the suffering of mothers and infants, through the centuries. The poet is left to beg of her muse the words to witness what she has apprehended. The title poem is the heart of the book, but not perhaps its finest moment.

The last poem is a superb one about the mad Charles V1 of France, who believed he was made from glass – a fitting emblem for the time, the poet feels. It ends with heartbreaking simplicity, in its portrayal of his Bavarian queen:

> an ordinary honest woman out of place
> in all this, wanting nothing more than the man
> she married, all her sorrows in her stolid face.
> ('The Glass King')

This is Boland, I think, at her finest. It is a thumbnail portrait, unadorned in its psychological acuity, the plain vocabulary mirroring the point. The lineation, the caesura it requires and the quiet alliteration of the final line all contribute to its effect . As George D. Painter, writing of Proust forty plus years ago, observed, 'the true function of the imagination is, paradoxically, not to imagine – in the sense of inventing or transforming – but to see: to see the reality which is concealed by habit and the phenomenal world.' The portrait 'sees' the reality of the queen and her plight.

Outside History (1990) concerns the marginalised, the women whom history has not 'rescued' from the past, whose ordinary heroisms and hardships have happened unnoticed. Its justly popular opening poem, 'The Black Lace Fan My Mother Gave Me', is a fascinating, cinematic, imagined memoir of the poet's parents enduring a heat wave in pre-war Paris. Its conventional romanticism is undercut with images of suffering (the heat is 'killing', the tortoiseshell 'worn out'). The eroticism of the exotic object, the fan, is therefore subverted.

Boland's striking turn of phrase and image are everywhere apparent in *Outside History*. So, for example, of 'The Achill Woman' from whom the naïve poet turns, in order to study the poets of the Silver Age, she writes:

> I remember the cold rosiness of her hands.
> She bent down and blew on them like broth.

There is a history of hardship in the image, as well as the automatic creation of character.

In '*On the Gift of* The Birds of America *by John James Audubon*' the poet writes of the tern's plummeting:

> the franchise of light these camphor-coloured wings opened out
> once with and are at such a loss for now, ...

evoking in the line both right and privilege, colour and smell – in fact, recalling the magisterial book itself.

In 'Mountain Time' light is again the source of imagery:

> the arc of the salmon after sudden capture –
> its glitter a larceny of daylight on slate.

In both poems the juxtaposition of law and light is startling. Unusual images make the domestic memorable, also. In 'Hanging Curtains with an Abstract Pattern in a Child's Room', for instance:

> my skirt the colour of
> all the disappointments of a day when
>
> the curtains are pulled back on
> a dull morning.

Similarly, in 'Distances' a busy market offers:

> linen for sale and tacky apples, and a glass and wire hill
> of spectacles on a metal tray.

Here the 'tacky' is tactile as well as shoddy, underlining in its other sense the vulgarity of the comical heap of glasses.

Throughout the collection, natural and domestic worlds are rendered in such sudden colours and light. Clearly, light is Evan Boland's medium. In *Outside History* she seems most at her ease; the poems invest the domestic with true symbolic power. Thematically, the book centres on the poet's commitment:

> I have chosen:
>
> out of myth into history I move to be
> part of that ordeal
> whose darkness is
>
> only now reaching me from those fields,
> those rivers, those roads clotted as
> firmaments with the dead.
> ('Outside History')

Myth has served her well, but is ultimately blank-faced. There is pain in plenty, but by definition it is timeless and therefore less than human.

The domestic poems in this fine collection are generally quiet, turning on an image, soaked in memory, love, dusk and light. To pause over 'Contingencies', 'Midnight Flowers', 'A Different Light' or 'Distances', say, is to be moved by special moments, such as those we live yet often miss.

The equally impressive, *In a Time of Violence*, came out in 1994. Boland described her intention at the time:

These are poems about Ireland, about the body, about growing older in both and using each as a text for the other. The time of violence in the title happens in the present and in the past. It happens in the soul and in the event.

The sequence, 'Writing in a Time of Violence', takes its moment from Plato's idea of the poet implanting 'an evil constitution', in his irrationality. It focuses on Irish language and history, from the conflagration of eighteenth century dissent, the 'famine roads' of 1847, the lot of Irish seamstresses. 'The Doll's Museum in Dublin', for instance, is a unique meditation on this emblem of the cosseted.

In the poem, 'Time and Violence', we are with marginalised women again, women as object in the lyric tradition (a shepherdess, Cassiopeia, a mermaid). They are wounded, defeated, ensnared by language. They beg for their mortality. This is put most succinctly in the final poem, 'A Woman Painted on a Leaf', with the cry, 'Let me die'.

Also, there is still the old nagging sense of the poet as outsider in her own land ('In Which the Ancient History I Learn Is Not My Own'), of being estranged from tradition, a sadness time cannot dull:

The nation which eludes me.

Fractions of a life
It has taken me a lifetime
To claim.   ('Anna Liffey')

Edna Longley argued, in 'The Living Stream' (1994), that in a recent pamphlet, Boland unquestioningly and unwisely held 'to unitary assumptions about a society, a nation, a literary heritage'. This is an interesting point and, if it is a weakness in Boland's work, it is also a strength, because the sense of one nation, one tradition, is at the heart of her vision, whatever the reality. I would argue that that vision of Ireland stems at least in part from her sense of exile – as the poem above suggests – and has led to a commitment, which is part desire. It also gives her poetry its power and her language its vitality.

New Collected Poems ends with the two books which have followed her 1995 *Collected Poems: The Lost Land* (1998) and *Code* (2001). The land in question is, the poet explains, 'the ghostly territory where so much human experience comes to be stored.' Though it may be neither country nor state of mind, its key note is nevertheless – and characteristically – exile. It explores the consequences of:

> a passionate economy
> we call the past. Although
> its other name may be memory
> ('Watching Old Movies When They Were New')

In 'Colony', part one of the collection, the poet refutes the notion of poetry as 'a gentle art' ('My Country in Darkness'), invoking the ghosts of the 'unhealed' past, the 'dispossessed':

> Out of my mouth they come.
> The spurred and booted garrisons.
> The men and women
> they dispossessed.
> ('Witness')

The second sequence, 'The Lost Land', involves America. *'Ireland. Absence. Daughter'* are its lament, as the poet revisits her childhood, the myth of the grieving mother, Ceres, and the growing of her daughters.

Code brings Eavan Boland's story up-to-date. The book is again dedicated to her husband, its first part celebrating their marriage. As she writes in the prose of 'Against Love Poetry':'I did not find my womanhood in the servitudes of custom. But I saw my humanity look back at me there.'

These poems eschew the absurdities within the tradition of love poetry, choosing to celebrate instead:

> the code marriage makes of passion –
> duty dailyness routine
> ('Thankëd be Fortune')

The preoccupation with the domestic is not a reduction of ambition, for she is still at other times a fiercely romantic poet. Otherwise Kings and Irish wolves and the 'bitter fire' of constellations would not continue to light her pages – nor would a simple roof leak, in 'Lines for a Thirtieth Wedding Anniversary', allow

> Through it, rain which came from the east,
> in from the lights and foghorns of the coast,
> water with a ghost of ocean salt in it,
> spilled down on the path below.

In the second part of the book, the codes are various: calligraphy, computers, money, crockery, emigrant letters, memory and so on. There are welcome versions of Horace and Pushkin, and a moment which, after nine volumes of poetry, give the reader pause:

>   what we see is how
>   the place and the torment of the place are
>   for this moment free of one another.
>   ('How We Made a New Art on Old Ground')

It is hard to believe that this poet sees, even for a moment, an Irish landscape free of 'the torment of the place'.

Eavan Boland's themes are richly mined by now – womanhood, identity, suffering, the Irish past – but she writes so well and so urgently that one is interested to see variations on such serious issues. Indeed, what one takes away from *New Collected Poems* is the recognition that Boland continues to explore, with memorable lyricism, 'the meeting place between womanhood and history', and indeed expands beyond themes relating to womanhood where she writes androgynously with strength and music. Time will tell whether she will 'detonate' into the consciousness as deeply as Plath, Rich and Bishop. Certainly, her stature is considerable.

Two Poems on John Clare

Robert Etty

I kicked it out of the clods,

John Clare said when they asked him where
his poetry came from, how someone so
unschooled from somewhere so unvisited
had learnt the things he seemed to know:

and in rushes at Helpstone snipe were
hiding, a vixen at dusk set up squealing;
the sky was streaked with grey to the west
and the earth was itself the feeling.

Robert Hamberger

From Heading North

(John Clare's *Journey out of Essex*)

In July 1841 John Clare escaped from High Beach asylum in Epping Forest, where he had been treated as an in-patient for four years. He walked over eighty miles in four days home to Northamptonshire.

Escape

July 18th 1841. Sunday. Felt very melancholy – went a walk in the forest in the afternoon – fell in with some gypsies, one of whom offered to assist in my escape from the madhouse.

>Am I coming or going?
>When you dawdle under beech-leaves this evening
>look both ways like mother said.
>
>The red road or the white one?
>Unhinge myself. Unhook this sack of stones,
>walking out on a trail of breadcrumbs through the wood.
>
>Am I coming or going? The red road or the white?
>They're open as a woman's legs:
>run after lines until your ink goes dry.
>
>Nuts and berries patter on my plate.
>Eat escape, eat it before the trap shuts.
>Why do you wait?
>
>I'm too blind for the journey.
>Mother it's getting dark. Mister say which way.

Man and Boy

On the left hand side the road under the bank like a cave I saw a man and boy coiled up asleep, which I hailed and they woke up to tell me the name of the next village.

The boy speaks:

>We coil like day-old pups. No milk. No mother.
>I nuzzle his beard's thicket,
>hook thumbs through his greatcoat buttonholes, hanging on.
>
>Some stoop under slate or thatch all winter,
>so I beg them. Does wind clack teeth
>and prickle their napes like mine?
>
>I'll bite a farthing to clap those crows away.
>When I scraped this dug-out deeper
>he laughed me his little workhorse and roughed my hair.
>
>Your yell kept pecking at my eardrums.
>Father names a place to make you happy.
>Mother's voice fades again the second I wake.

Here's Another

A man passed me on horseback in a slop-frock and said 'here's another of the broken-down haymakers' and threw me a penny to get a half pint of beer, which I picked up and thanked him for.

He speaks:

>Being a high man astride a bay-mare
>my voice counts for something down this street,
>when I'm luckier than loose change in a pocket
>and the saddle's steady, the hooves slow.
>
>I note cloud-smoke and attic windows,
>ponder the poor below: how many,
>how my horse could slap dung onto waiting hands.
>
>Here's another, broken as a bulrush,
>his whipped look kindling a penny's pity.
>Perhaps. Compassion learns its limits.
>
>Mark my fidget between embarrassment and pleasure
>when he dips his neck like a wag-tail,
>his tongue a weathered flail I barely hear.

Lace

I called in a house to light my pipe in which was a civil old woman and a young country wench making lace on a cushion as round as a globe.

She speaks:

>Windmills, brides and butterflies
>rise from my pillow.
>
>Fingers twist our living until candlelight:
>pennies a yard, shillings a week.
>
>I'll weave a snow kiss when it's warranted,
>squint at bobbins whatever questions come
>
>from the journeyman who sucks his pipe on our doorstep,
>this maze under my knuckles a lover's knot.

A Tall Gypsy

I saw a tall gypsy come out of the lodge gate and make down the road ... I got up and went on to the next town with her. She cautioned me on the way to put something in my hat to keep the crown up and said in a lower tone 'You'll be noticed,' but not knowing what she hinted I took no notice and made no reply.

She speaks:

> I live this skin, wanting no other:
> not to be some milk-face supping indoors.
> They quake politely when I read their smiles
> as if I'll blab which husband bores, who dies tomorrow.
>
> We side with each other
> for ten furlongs into town,
> talk of heading north and why swifts won't land
> before I warn his gawky look.
>
> Ape them or you'll be noticed.
> Straighten your hat. Stiffen its crown
> and you can skip their questions.
> Take a short cut. Drop the road you're on.

Poor Creature

A young woman (so I guessed by the voice) came out of a house and said 'poor creature' and another more elderly said 'O he shams.' But when I got up the latter said 'O no he don't', as I hobbled along very lame.

Young woman:

>   There but for the grace of God
>   I stumble, lie exhausted
>   as this scarcely man who shuts his eyes
>   for sleep and peace won't come.
>
>   Less than a fly fussing on a leaf
>   and still alive.
>
>   Should I comfort,
>   offer him a woman's outstretched hand?
>   He lifts his bag of bones again,
>   walks past us both as if he limps through flame.

Neighbours From Helpstone

A man and woman passed me in a cart and on hailing me as they passed I found they were neighbours from Helpstone where I used to live – I told them I was knocked up which they could easily see and that I had neither ate nor drank any thing since I left Essex. When I told my story they clubbed together and threw me fivepence out of the cart.

The man speaks:

>We sprouted in the same back garden:
>him a dog rose, me a bramble
>but I've always fed my children.
>Can he say as much?
>
>Poetry's a wet harvest.
>Look at him. I knew he'd end up useless,
>his way with words
>enough to skin a pebble, nothing more.
>
>Do we cart him home?
>Now he's daft there's no knowing.
>He could eat us in our sleep.
>Click the reins. Best leave him where he is.
>
>His story shakes our pennies.
>We throw five and watch him grub the dust.
>When he's miles behind
>I keep hearing his children call us back.

The Woman

When nearing me the woman jumped out and caught fast hold of my hands and wished me to get into the cart but I refused and thought her either drunk or mad. But when I was told it was my second wife Patty I got in and was soon at Northborough.

Patty speaks:

> He blathers Mary like a love-whipped boy.
> He's blind to me. My scorched man,
> too long in the sun. If it rained
> who licked drops off his lashes,
> promised him tomorrow would be dry?
>
> Four years waiting and still no cure
> but I can mend him: patch his elbows,
> rest the shade of fingers over his eyes.
>
> I sang him asleep after the children,
> drunk from his wooing and glad to be so.
> Even now, squeezing his hands again,
> saying my name until he remembers
> I wake foot to finger at his side.

Edward Ragg

Chosen young Broadsheet essayist, 29, is a poet and wine consultant. A former Fellow of the Rothermere American Institute, Oxford, he holds a Ph.D. in English from Cambridge where he taught from 2001-2006. His poetry and criticism have appeared in many international journals. He is currently co-editing, with Bart Eeckout, a collection of essays entitled *Wallace Stevens across the Atlantic*. He will shortly set up a wine consultancy in Beijing, China.

Abstraction and its Detractors: Wallace Stevens in the 21st Century

In August 2005 Bart Eeckhout and I co-organized 'Fifty Years On: Wallace Stevens in Europe', an international conference coinciding with the month of Stevens's death a half-century ago. The event was hosted by the Rothermere American Institute, Oxford University; and gathered together scholars, editors, poets and other enthusiasts to discuss Stevens's legacy in light of his relations with European arts, culture and letters.

The Oxford event was inspired by two 2004 gatherings: a substantial University of Connecticut conference organized by Glen MacLeod and Charles Mahoney; and a smaller symposium at the University of London assembled by Josh Cohen. Those gatherings had marked the fiftieth anniversary of the Knopf edition of Stevens's *Collected Poems*. The Oxford event, honouring the appearance of the 1955 Faber *Collected*, asked some soul-searching questions about whether Stevens is alive and well today, not least for British poetry readers.

Certainly, the reception and criticism of Stevens's work is largely an American affair. On the volume of critical literature, this is indisputable. In fact, Stevens is sufficiently popular in academic circles that US doctoral theses on the poet outnumber those produced on other American modernist poets. Looking beyond the US, some American scholars have spoken of a British resistance to Stevens. But such resistance presupposes familiarity; and we should not underestimate how, even with increased transatlantic dialogue, poetry cultures will remain, to some extent, regional and national even as they are influenced internationally. In short, while American poetry continues to have the enduring influence on British verse, and a British poetry audience, it discovered in the second-half of the 20th century, there

---

[1] See 'Stevens and British Literature' *The Wallace Stevens Journal* ed. Bart Eeckhout and Edward Ragg 30.1 Spring 2006. Selected papers from the Oxford conference have also appeared in *PN Review* 169.

is not necessarily a British conspiracy afoot to leave Stevens out of the equation (and it was, after all, T. S. Eliot who was tellingly slow to publish the poet at Faber).

Fortunately, Stevens is known to British readers thanks to the early attempts of Nicholas Moore and Anne Ridler to publish the poet. In the panoply of major 20th century critics, most of whom cut their teeth on Stevens at formative stages of their own careers (Vendler, Bloom, Hillis Miller, Frye, Altieri), there are also eloquent non-North Americans like Frank Kermode and Denis Donoghue, both of whom recognized the importance of Stevens's work early on (as did Al Alvarez). So the Oxford conference capitalised on the enthusiasm for Stevens that already exists outside the US, particularly in Europe and Britain; an interest hardly derived from American criticism alone.

Admittedly, that interest is far from pervasive, even within the relatively small readerships of the poetry world. But measuring poets' importance by volume is misplaced (which is why statistics about doctoral dissertations only tell a partial story). Certainly, a contemporary British poetry audience is aware of Stevens's significance, whether he is resisted, welcomed or even shrugged off. After all, Stevens's influence on a variety of 20th century poetries is undeniable, even if, outside the US, figures like Williams, O'Hara or Ashbery might crop up in conversation first; all poets who are actually related to Stevens in various ways (one could add Cummings, Kees, Lowell, Roethke, Berryman, Plath, Merrill and Justice).

As for the non-American poets, David Gascoyne, W. H. Auden (both before and after becoming an American citizen), Charles Tomlinson, Peter Redgrove, R. S. Thomas, Hugh MacDiarmid, Norman MacCaig, Seamus Heaney and, more recently, James Fenton, Mark Ford, Matthew Welton, Patrick Mackie and Jeremy Over are just some of those to have responded to Stevens; although, as I will explain, the ambivalence over Stevens can be as revealing as the overtures.

But we should not forget the struggles Stevens's reputation underwent in America itself during the 1920s and '30s: mixed reviews that were replicated in Britain and whose echoes can still be heard today. The poet of *Harmonium* (1923) was dismissed as a talented dandy, when most commentators were following the international careers of Eliot and Pound (or admiring Frost's more 'accessible' poetic). Stevens also played little part in forging his own reputation; at least, he refrained from the self-promotion Whitman exhibited before him and Pound always had in spades. Unlike Marianne Moore or Williams, Stevens wrote little literary journalism; and he never edited a little magazine. Apart from early contact with the Arensberg circle, Stevens eschewed literary and artistic groups, particularly once ensconced in Hartford, Conn., pursuing his career as a surety bond lawyer.

Thus, like Thoreau – although without the Transcendentalist bent – Stevens was essentially a stay-at-home poet who rarely travelled outside the US and never came to Europe. As Dana Gioia has commented, this was remarkable for someone of Stevens's social rank: revealing the security of environment the poet required to produce poetry as well as order his own life. Even Williams had travelled to Paris and met Joyce before feeling betrayed by Eliot's seeming denial of America and 'Americanness'. Stevens, by contrast, only left Hartford to give the occasional lecture or to meet up with his long-term New York friends, Barbara and Henry Church.

But Stevens's reputation in the US would grow as interest in Eliot waned around the time the New Critical revolution had elapsed and the study of Romantic poetry underwent a much-needed revival. Previously, Stevens had been under-read and under-valued by Cleanth Brooks and Co. because of his 'Romanticism' and his quirky French tendencies (the poet's absorption of French Symbolism was, for the New Critics, not as refined as Eliot's).

Moreover, Stevens's work never fitted a modernist paradigm neatly; and it is best read, if one needs a paradigm, as straddling modernist and postmodernist concerns. Despite their critical preferences, figures like Allen Tate and John Crowe Ransom would have to engage with Stevens; and there is considerable evidence they admired his work – Ransom even overcoming his distaste for 'abstraction' by praising the 'philosophical position' of 'Notes Toward a Supreme Fiction' (1942), despite its provocative first section: *'It Must Be Abstract'*. Stevens also published regularly in the *Kenyon*, *Sewanee* and *Southern* reviews. So he was not overlooked: he was just an unlikely champion for the New Criticism. The poet's reputation also grew slowly because he wrote his best poetry in the last twenty years of his long life (from 1935-55). Thus, both in America and Britain, it was not until the 1960s that Stevens's reputation could be consolidated.

There is also the problem of a bias to the early work: many of Stevens's readers still preferring *Harmonium* to anything else the poet wrote. But the most anthologized pieces – 'The Snow Man', 'Sunday Morning', 'Anecdote of the Jar', all from *Harmonium* – are only parts of Stevens's accomplishment. While Stevens himself borrowed heavily from his first book in assembling his Knopf and Faber *Selected Poems*, it is to *The Man with the Blue Guitar* (1937), *Parts of a World* (1942), *Transport to Summer* (1947), *The Auroras of Autumn* (1950) and the last section of the *Collected Poems*, 'The Rock' (1954), that committed readers of Stevens turn. And there's the rub: it is in Stevens's post-*Harmonium* work that the poet has traditionally lost a readership (American or British). The work after *Harmonium* is still less well-known – with the exception of perhaps 'Notes' and the late lyrics – and is often considered less hospitable. This has much to do with the increasingly abstract spirit of the Stevens corpus.

So what's wrong with abstraction? In Connecticut 2004, Christian Wiman complained that Stevens's poems can often seem removed, lacking in feeling: too engaged with the idea of 'reality' rather than with the 'actual world' the poet had strained toward during the Depression. The charge of coldness has been aired before: James Fenton suggesting that unhappiness does not seem to have been a colour in Stevens's palette. In those early *Harmonium* reviews, Stevens was characterized as verbally brilliant, but lacking much, if anything, to say (a playboy of the Western Word, as one critic quipped). Since then, resourceful critics like Vendler have been quick to focus upon the frustrated desires in Stevens's work. But it is undeniably true that what readers look for in Harrison, Larkin, Reading or Berryman, they are not likely to find in Stevens. No wonder Ted Hughes could not get past the poet's 'magniloquence'; and even Seamus Heaney admits to struggling with 'that great cloudscape of language'. Perhaps, to borrow Stevens's own language, his work can appear unnervingly ethereal: "It is a theatre floating through the clouds, / Itself a cloud, although of misted rock / And mountains running like water, wave on wave/ Through waves of light" ('The Auroras of Autumn' VI, 1948).

But Stevens is actually an easier poet to pick up than might appear; and, as Milton J. Bates suggests, sympathetic critics need not fill in the gaps unsympathetic critics decry (while unsympathetic readers can simply read someone else). The point of Stevensian abstraction is to re-create one's sense of 'reality'. Like Proust and Beckett, the poet desires to strip away the veneer of inherited ideas and habit, hence all the talk in 'Notes' of seeing the world as an ignorant man: to be a thinker of the 'first idea'. In brief, Stevens does not invite readers to feel with him, but rather, as Paul Valéry argues in 'Poetry and Abstract Thought' (1939), to communicate 'a poetic state' (Valéry being an important precedent for Stevens). That state depends on drawing the reader into an abstract speculation both on poetry and the poetic:

> The poem is the cry of its occasion,
> Part of the res itself and not about it.
> The poet speaks the poem as it is,
>
> Not as it was: part of the reverberation
> Of a windy night as it is, when the marble statues

>   Are like newspapers blown by the wind.
>   ('An Ordinary Evening in New Haven' XII, 1949)

Moreover, anyone interested in the New York School or the way in which American poetry was shaped by Cubism and Abstract Expressionism should find Stevens compelling. He's not a verbal Rothko or Pollock; but his diction is classically hard to 'see' (Stevens implies in 'The Creations of Sound' [1944] that poetry should 'make the visible a little hard / To see'). Indeed, his poems are abstracted notions of what a poem might be. As Williams said of 'The Man with the Blue Guitar', Stevens was adept in writing 'virtual lyrics':

> Poetry is the subject of the poem,
> From this the poem issues and
>
> To this returns. Between the two,
> Between issue and return, there is
>
> An absence in reality,
> Things as they are. Or so we say.
>   ('The Man with the Blue Guitar' XXII, 1937).

This makes Stevens ripe for citation. His rising popularity in interdisciplinary contexts (he is probably the most quoted but under-read poet of his generation) as well as his lodestar-status for poets like Jorie Graham, Susan Howe and Mark Doty, indicates an on-going fascination: one that his abstract and self-reflexive diction has actually encouraged.

But it would be better to let Stevens speak more fully for himself by quoting the end of that painterly poem 'Landscape With Boat' (1940). Here Stevens jostles the values and limits of abstract meditation, creating an idiom that mixes humility with imaginative reach, cultivating a Europe he would only discover through correspondence and picture postcards:

> Had he been better able to suppose:
> He might sit on a sofa on a balcony
> Above the Mediterranean, emerald
> Becoming emeralds. He might watch the palms
> Flap green ears in the heat. He might observe
> A yellow wine and follow a steamer's track
> And say, "The thing I hum appears to be
> The rhythm of this celestial pantomime."

For Stevens knew, in fact, the dangers of imaginative solipsism; but he had learnt from Cézanne and Picasso that there could be no purely abstract art (just as, as Stanley Fish would argue, no one can actively be a solipsist).

From roughly 1940 to the end of his career Stevens absorbed this abstractive spirit and made it his own, even as his later poetry turns to a more 'personal' idiom:

> His place, as he sat and as he thought, was not
> In anything that he constructed, so frail,
> So barely lit, so shadowed over and naught,
>
> As, for example, a world in which, like snow,
> He became an inhabitant, obedient
> To gallant notions on the part of cold.
>
> ('A Quiet Normal Life', c. 1954)

With luck, the great poetry of Stevens's late and last years should discover an on-going international interest in the next fifty years and beyond.

Edward Ragg

Owl and Cat: A Lesson

'These forms are not abortive figures, rocks,
Impenetrable symbols, motionless. They move

About the night.'
              – Wallace Stevens, 'The Owl in the Sarcophagus'

Bookshelves and spines: nouns of the celebrated dead
Now gold once more as the lamps of the classroom shine,
As the afternoon light thins and, fading, plays;

That passage from Shelley's *Defence*, our tired faces
Stretched far from those 'eternal regions' where the
'Owl-winged faculty of calculation dare never soar',

As if the poet stood in the corner fuming, in one hand
A tattered manuscript, in the other a bird of prey;
The silence as our brows crumple, our eyelids fall.

Then the long walk home where the lamps gleam
Bumper to bumper and the winter moon surveys
Its obvious tenure, unwatched and new.

Suddenly, in a familiar street an owl calls. I stand
Stiller than the black cat who pauses on a fence
And listens, as if by pausing here all three of us

Could elope and sail away for a year and a day,
As if with runcible spoons we might eat our fills
Or the cat and owl lullaby under my moon-like gaze.

This is not dark scholar's bird, half-moon specs surveying
A tawny breast, no more than cat must be Egyptian deity.
Owl, hint your hooting: only you pronounce *magnificat*.

Robert Stein

What Should Modern Poetry Do?

A book on 20th century poetry raises some fundamental questions

Colin Falck's bracingly-written book *American and British verse in the 20th century: the poetry that matters*[1] argues, at a time when such polemics are unfashionable, that some modern poetry matters and some does not and that the criterion for judging which does is tied to the view of poetry as a spiritual enterprise of revelation – that poetry is the best medium for understanding and shaping human experience. Poems that use their resources of vocabulary, metre, rhyme and subject-matter so that 'ordinarily educated people' can enjoy and perhaps even remember them – and return to read them for pleasure – are those that matter. Modernism and experimentalism have their place: Falck's canon includes Robinson Jeffers, Peter Reading, Auden and Hart Crane before *The Bridge*, but poetry written (as he sees it) for an over-literary audience does not.

Falck argues his case well, in an intelligent, thoughtful and engaging tone that, appropriately, the 'ordinarily educated' reader will relish. If the basis for his position sounds like more than the two-centuries old Romantic philosophy of Wordsworth, Coleridge and their fellow-travellers in Germany and elsewhere, then Falck sees this only as a truth that has sadly been drowned out since the publication of *Lyrical Ballads*. Whatever one may think of the argument, it is surely good news that the question is put squarely in front of us: what is modern poetry for? Furthermore, does poetry matter only if it bears this revelatory burden?

I am doubtful. We ought to feel suspicious of the grander claims made for poets such as Shelley's that they are the 'unacknowledged legislators of the world' or, as again Falck quotes with satisfaction, Pound's boast that he and others were the 'antennae of the race'. As the ancient proverb reminds us 'If triangles had a God, He'd have three sides' and almost every profession – philosophers, psychotherapists, priests – vainly see themselves as having privileged access to the truth. They would, wouldn't they? In the free market of our time, all of the above callings need the status that such insight would confer.

The problem with the argument is that it is seductive because – like religion – it is partly correct. There are lines, stanzas and whole poems that are so reflective, so satisfyingly summative of human experience that

---

[1] Colin Falck *American and British verse in the 20th century: the poetry that matters* (Ashgate, 2003)

it is natural to look to all poetry for this same profound pleasure. An example of the opposing – look to the result, not the content – argument is Emily Dickinson's claim, interestingly coming from one of the great precursors of modernism, that 'If I feel physically as if the top of my head were taken off, I know that is poetry'. This sounds intuitively appealing too, but only shows that there is no single formula for defining what poetry should do, or which poems succeed in this aim.

A more serious difficulty is the assumption that poetry has – or should have – a single aim. Allied to this is the confusion between the ostensible aim of a poem and that poem's success in achieving it. A poem such as Donne's 'At the round earth's imagined corners' has as its goal the demonstration of God's magnificence using dazzling conceits as a principal technique; but the small relevance of its aim to the modern world does not diminish the power of its metaphors.

I would argue too that the acknowledged diversity of twentieth-century poetry in particular points not only to divergences in technique and subject-matter but to a more fundamental divergence among poets as to what they see the purposes of their work being. A consideration of the work of just three poets of the 1960s: say Robert Creeley, Adrian Henri and Philip Larkin might lead one to wonder whether any preface to a book of this decade could be so broad in its poetic philosophy as to embrace the outlook of such disparate writers.

Not that this is an argument for the sixties' own notorious many-things go so anything-goes approach. The fact that poetry was and remains incorrigibly plural in recent times only means that there are more ways for the individual poem to fail, not that one can always find some yardstick by which it succeeds. That's one sixties attitude we are better off without.

*

Of all English-language poets of the 20th century, the one whose enduring status provides the greatest challenge to Falck's central argument is Wallace Stevens. The characters in Stevens' poems, whether they are the emperor of ice cream or take tea at the Palaz of Hoon are deliberately, proudly, fanciful. What is more, Stevens' diction, self-consciously confident, witty, learned and glorifying both in sensuality and abstraction makes him such an exemplar of all that the modern poet – according to Falck – should not be that he claims his abstraction-driven work is 'not modern poetry at all'. Yet in many ways Stevens' work is modernist *par excellence*, not only in its playful self-obsession with the role of art in modern consciousness but in its glitteringly opulent vocabulary. Falck wonders if there is any reason behind this 'bizarre Frenchified language'. Consider the opening of 'Evening without angels.'

> Why seraphim like lutanists arranged
> Above the trees? And why the poet as
> Eternal *chef d'orchestre*?
> > Air is air,
>
> Its vacancy glitters round us everywhere.
> Its sounds are not angelic syllables
> But our unfashioned spirits realized
> More sharply in more furious selves.
>
> > And light
> That fosters seraphim and is to them
> Coiffeur of haloes, fecund jeweller –

Imagine *chef d'orchestre* replaced with either 'leader of the orchestra' or, for Americans, 'concertmaster', and see how inelegant, how workaday the line becomes. And what about that coiffured description of light as 'Coiffeur of haloes, fecund jeweller…'? Stevens' ubiquitous Frenchification is an appropriate linguistic trope. French, to the Anglophone imagination, is the language of seductiveness, refinement and sensual delight. Stevens' use of it mirrors his view of poetry and all art as itself providing the sustaining beauty, pleasure and ritual formerly to be found in the discredited myths of religion. Like the Metaphysicals, those other traffickers in metaphorical abstractions, Stevens needs a surprisingly excessive diction and pungent sensuousness to bring within our grasp otherwise inaccessible philosophical concepts.

Stevens is a difficult poet, but unlike some justifiably-denigrated writers, the invented vocabulary and the Surrealist-style rhyming in, for example, 'Anything is beautiful if you say it is' actually serve to amuse, to seduce us to consider arguments that we might not normally make.

It is true that there is much artificiality and indifference to or rejection of ordinary human life in Stevens' oeuvre, but no more than we might find in, say, George Herbert, although the latter's quarrel with human appetites had different motives. Poetry may start its commerce 'in the foul rag-and-bone shop of the heart' but there is no reason why it should not end its dealings elsewhere.

Reactions to John Ashbery, the prolific presiding spirit of post-modernist poetry, are an indicator of how one regards the contemporary scene. Unashamedly a recondite poet, Ashbery nevertheless presents a very different persona in his work to Stevens. If the former is a fastidious aesthete much-travelled in Europe, Stevens is essentially a New Yorker out on the streets who rambles on, sometimes losing his train of thought but never letting you forget that art and the difficulties of creating art are something that he knows all about. His tone is summed up by Falck as '... mirror[ing] the expressionless theory-attenuated speech ... in which almost anything can be entertained or analysed as a possibility.' It lacks focus, it is inwardly intellectual, hell it can be *annoying*.

Beyond this initial recoil that many feel, the more serious case against Ashbery – and one that Falck makes cogently – is how his poems largely evade or eschew human perceptions or experience altogether in favour of a continual riffing on the idea of the difficulties of communicating at all.

Wilful obscurity is the fifth columnist of the avant-garde, damaging the reputation of its sincere practitioners, and Ashbery at his worst can do a lot of damage. At his best though, Ashbery's technique resembles Joyce's in *Ulysses* insofar as his authorial attention is simultaneously on language, on his own self and the imagined lives of others: at once self-consciously static and ever-reaching towards greater understandings. No wonder the reader gets frustrated at times. But like Joyce, Ashbery's poems do have a goal, even if it is proceeded towards circuitously. *Pace* Falck, Ashbery's typical strategy for a poem is actually to make headway out of all the confusion and uncertainty, so a sub-text might run, 'There's a feeling that I wish to communicate, and I can't put it into words easily. So here's an anecdote or a glimpse of something that feels relevant, here's a more abstract attempt to say it; but now I am distracted by some other stuff. OK, let me start again on another tack, perhaps that doesn't work either. Look, I'm not sure myself, maybe it's a bit like this.'

In other words Ashbery isn't *celebrating* – as his detractors suggest – difficulties of communication so much as *trying*, right in front of our eyes, to make sense of aspects of experience that resist our attempts to understand or define them. In his poem 'Street Musicians', a trio breaks up following the death of one member, and the second's soul is 'wrenched out' as he wanders the streets. The third '... beached/Glimpses of what the other was up to:/Revelations at last...'. The poet, in a typically parallel situation, admits to an only partial understanding of his own motives and imperfect technique with which to express them. He 'cradles this average violin'. Nevertheless, he, like all of us, betrays a restless urge for self-understanding:

> Our question of a place of origin hangs
> Like smoke: how we picnicked in pine forests,
> In coves with the water always seeping up, and left
> Our trash, sperm and excrement everywhere, smeared
> On the landscape, to make of us what we could.

Helen Vendler[2] reads this as a poem about art, specifically a retort to Eliot's notion of the grand tradition of poetic lineage. Ashbery conversely rejoices, she claims, Duchamp-like in the task of manufacture out of life's ready-mades.

And yet for all Ashbery's lofty confidence in 'an obscure family being evicted/ into the way it was, and is...', the poem's tentative conclusion and the ordinariness of its picnicking image make it rather a poem – to use another Eliot image – of 'fragments shored against the ruins': here are our instinctive attempts to make meanings in our lives, to make ourselves, not the world, 'tuneful', despite 'increasingly suburban airs' and equipped only with imperfect instruments.

Falck would have you believe that the *sine qua non* for poetry mattering in the present time is its being written in a language that reconnects poetry 'with everyday life as we ordinarily live it' but this is to confuse honesty with simplicity. The feeling that poetry should connect strongly with our lives sounds almost political, and this is no accident. The one-line section that concludes the book reads in its entirety, 'The poets have only interpreted the world. The point still remains: to change it.' Seen that way, poetry looks like Marxism, the other god, after God, that failed. Surely poetry matters more, and more variously, than its function to point us towards that longed-for landscape, however appealing.

---

[2] Helen Vendler 'Ashbery's Aesthetic: Reporting on Fairfield Porter and Saul Steinberg' *Harvard Review* No. 22 (Spring 2002)

John Haynes

Spirit Possession

For Afiniki Kyari
(part of a long sequence)

XXXIV

And here's a soul? Pure light. Whose back is turned.
Whose plaits are bunched up with a clip. A gold
earring, a glasses' frame, a cheek outlined
against a cabinet of pale brown panelled
wood. No eyes, no face, to tell how old
the subject is. We'd have to wait until
she turns to face us, as she never will.

Except it seems to me you were about
to turn, had felt my lens on you, had paused
for it to click, the flash to shiver out,
the moment go, not wanting to be caught
full on, full in the face, or so I thought
if I recall it, fixed like this, the moment,
as it was, as I imagine it.

I told you this is all just empathy,
out of those *mirror cells* down in the sub-
cortex, the lizard brain, *the pulmonary
variations* on the theme of lub
and dub. The comic strip balloons come up
and stir the air towards you from my mouth.
Already they're half ink as they reach out.

XXXV

All panto minstrelsy and crumply tights,
the window lit up in the stone, the lute
to make the changes on and tune a sigh
to fret and interval, and make a *you*
out of the *you* vibrating in the gut
and throat and fingertips – which all connive
to sound as simple as the blackbirds' cry

just when the blue-black comes into the sky
above the front door where he waves the tinking
trafficators off, holding the coffee
still hot in his fist, something she thinks
that there's no need to do at all, something
to do with just that need, some prepschool boy's
drilled reassurance in brave-eyed goodbyes,

or shape a gesture in the air that's still
a shape for loneliness, the troubadour
in him, that has to find the outer style
and out of that devise his metaphor
of who she is, and what he's singing for,
that she'll hear in his voice, perhaps, or won't
perhaps, or he will for her if she can't.

XXXVI

Or else, instead, just drive her into work -
sharing the lady with the lollypop
and shining butter coat, kids at the kerb,
the lights on early in the paper shop,
the wheeling town and ocean from the top
of Portsdown Hill, and then the hospital,
the car slamming, her quick look back and smile.

Such small goodbyes and goings out of sight,
like Tristan's hand lifting beyond the hedge
as he runs off, come back sometimes at night
as I look back towards the shelves and fridge
from out there on the lawn beyond the edge
of panes projected on the grass, alone,
as timeless as time is, homeless as home

and just this sense of *here* itself is where
love can't comfort, for all that opiate
the village mallam[1] gave you to prepare
and sprinkle secretly onto my plate

---

[1] *mallam*: used colloquially in Hausa and N Nigerian English to mean 'medicine man'

of acha[1] in Kagoma[2] that time way
back when the trickster spirits nodded yes,
and without knowing what it was, I ate.

XXXVII

And no words words enough, or pictures. Scribble's
maybe closer to the helpless eyes
and stammerings, since it's not legible
and reaches for some limit speech denies
us with its own, towards a *paradise*[3]:
red finches, oranges, pools, glistening carp
through ripples like the shaking of a harp,

a voice, changing the boughs to metaphors
of its own sound, and claiming that is love.
Or is it fear – that boy's face in the grass
as Heinkel's mythic fighter[4] tips and dives
towards him in the dream, and that black glove's
poised just above the button as it came
and never came, again and yet again?

Or this garden. The bike left out, the pond
I dug and lined with plastic for the kids
where tadpoles coil and wriggle in a brown
they breathe a while among the waterweeds,
and are and aren't themselves, frogs no-one sees
although sometimes, too late, that splash behind
us makes us stop and try to catch the sound.

---

[1] *acha*: a kind of soup
[2] *Kagoma*: a village in Northern Nigeria near Jos
[3] paradise: also the Arabic word for 'garden'
[4] The Heinkel 100, redubbed 113, was publicised by Hitler's propagadists as a super performance fighter and it appeared in RAF recognition manuals etc, together with specially prepared realistic photographs, though it was never in fact produced despite having a higher perfomance than the famous Messerschmitt 109.

Duncan Sprott

Time Stopped

Thomas McCarthy, *Merchant Prince*, Anvil Press £11.95
John Seed, *New and Collected Poems*, Shearsman Books, £9.95
John Seed, *Pictures from Mayhew – London 1850*, Shearsman Books, £10.95
C.P. Cavafy, *I've Gazed So Much* – translations by George Economou, Stop Press, £8.95
C.P. Cavafy, *Collected Poems* – translated by Aliki Barnstone, Norton, £16.99

The common thread running through these five books is the past, and getting back the past. Thomas McCarthy's concern in *Merchant Prince* is a (semi-) fictional 18th/early 19th century past, put together with the utmost care, out of assorted fragments, and buoyed up by the kind of myriad minute authentic historical details that make us believe that his false world is true. His subtitle sums it up: *The life and passions of Nathaniel Murphy, gentleman-merchant, in Italy and Ireland.*
Murphy is a candidate for the priesthood, training in Rome, where he loses first his virginity, second his vocation, and third the family fortune, ending up as a Cork merchant. It's an interesting tale, with an interesting structure, for Murphy's first love is poetry, and he tells his story partly through his own poems. First we have *Blood* – 28 poems, then *Memory*, 105 pages of '18th century' prose, then *Trade*, 38 more poems. The poems are all dated – 1798, 1811, 1807 ... out of order, random, like memory itself, jumping back and forth in time, as Murphy unveils, relives and comes to terms with his history, his memories.

All the same, unravelling what McCarthy is up to is a complicated business. The initial chunk of poetry strikes one as oblique at first reading, referring at random to characters about whom we know nothing. Gradually, in the prose section, we can begin to separate the wood from the trees. Then we return to poetry with more eagerness, realising at last what the hell this is all about. This manipulation of the reader is an unusual feature of the book, and it's cleverly accomplished, because the effect is to hurry one straight back to the beginning, in search of answers to what was imperfectly understood first time round.

Difficulties do dog the reader, though. McCarthy peppers his prose with Italian, Latin, French, Irish Gaelic (*bozzetto, spailpín, amadán, tramoli, gubán saor*). McCarthy either thinks you should know what this lot means already, or wants you to find out for yourself. To be sure, McCarthy displays a prodigious knowledge of the historical topography of Cork city. But to the reader who does not happen to have the Mardyke, Montenotte, Passage (sc. Passage West, the Port of Cork) up his sleeve, those references will remain obscure. Much the same might be said of his treatment of Italy. McCarthy is on record as saying 'I don't write poems to confuse or complicate others. We all live at a slightly different wavelength from one another.' Tuning in to McCarthy's wavelength involves grappling with his constant allusion to four Italian poets – the Principessa Nulana Nigonelli, Limnio di Murthillo, Count Luigi da Pora, Giancarlo Oscharcighi – whose names happen to be near anagrams of living Irish poets – Nuala Ní Dhómhnaill, Liam O'Muirthile, Louis de Paor, Cathal Ó Searcaigh. It may be that crystal clear reception on this wavelength is not possible. The publisher's blurb calls this 'a complex book that reminds us we enjoy what we find the more because it was hidden.' Perhaps. *Merchant Prince* is a puzzle, requiring effort to solve: but that, and the sense that McCarthy is playing games, is what gives his book its fascination.

Instead of weaving the fragments of history into a seamless whole, John Seed's *New and Collected Poems* lets the fragments stand by themselves, stark, broken, telling. His trademark is the seemingly random selection of juxtaposed quotations, like soundbites from some great tape-recording of yesterday; like the echo of history, like Eliotic footfalls down the passage of time indeed. There is a compelling originality about the technique, but the randomness here can seem, well, just too random for comfort. These isolated gems are tantalizing, disjointed and obscure – like the past they describe and epitomize. Still, if this book sometimes fails to hold the attention, the cut and paste technique is triumphantly realised, in Seed's latest volume.

Pictures from Mayhew might look like no more than a scissors and paste job on Henry Mayhew's *London Labour and the London Poor* – but by deft editing and arranging, Seed has sharpened the focus and given us a sparkling and crackling fresh version of an almost forgotten masterpiece, in which the voices of the ordinary Londoners of 1850 were transcribed and preserved, like an exercise in stopping time. Sure, it was Henry Mayhew who captured these people speaking, but Seed's striking selection makes them jump to life. The result is moving, memorable, and, indeed, unputdownable.

What we are presented with is an arresting series of prose snapshots of the Victorian poor, hanging on to existence by the skin of their teeth. This stuff is the lost poetry of everyday life, the lost voice of history, and the voice is quite unlike anything heard today. Time changes, things move on, but in Seed/Mayhew the lost time is captured. Take, for example,

the red hot coke hauler who says the heat is 'fit to melt a man like a
roll of butter.' Or Shaking Jemmy, who earns a crust by shivering 'like
a calf's foot jelly with the ague.' Or the voice that says:

> I've stood
> up to the ankles in snow
> till after midnight &
> till I've wished I was
> snow myself & could melt &
> have an end

Or this one:

> I only wish I'd back
> all the money I've guv to the publican
> & I wouldn't care
> how the wind blew
> for the rest of my life

Or these words about the water supply:

> the water we use is
> we drink a solution of our own
> > faeces
> > dead dogs
> offal from slaughter-houses
> the entrails of animals
> pavement dirt stable dung night soil
> bodies of murdered men

Or this:

> *Asylum for the Houseless Poor Cripplegate dusk*
> *waiting shivering in the piercing wind cobwebby*
> *garments in tatters the shoeless keep one foot on*
> *the ground bare flesh blue on the snow*

Or this, of a Punch and Judy man:

> his name is writ
> in the annals of
> history & handed down
> as long as grass
> grows & water runs

The effect is charming and harrowing all at once, and utterly riveting. Seed says himself, 'I have cut and rearranged, sometimes feeling I was getting closer to the actual voices of these people in the streets of London 150 years ago.' He brings us very close.

Both McCarthy and Seed worry at the past, trying to hold on to, or get back, yesterday. Nobody, of course, does this better – or with greater poignancy – than Cavafy. George Economou's Cavafy translations in *I've Gazed So Much* are sharp and economical. He has chosen twenty-one poems of longing, desire, old desire, lost love and lovers. Always the leitmotif is regret for time gone by, time lost. We have here something of Cavafy's fascination for ancient Alexandria, revived, brought back to life. There's a good balance between the erotic, the historical, and the kind of poems that pack an emotional punch.

Cavafy has been so much worked over that it's difficult for any 'new' translation to look like anything but tinkering. In fact these translations do not differ wildly from the standard Keeley and Sherrard edition, but they do manage to avoid various awkwardnesses and infelicities. This is a worthy introduction, which should send anybody who is fresh to Cavafy in search of the complete works. The nineteen linocuts by Dieter Hall complement the poems admirably; nicely homoerotic, they capture something of the Cavafesque atmosphere, and have an interesting freshness and purity of line. One would like to see more – both of Economou's Cavafy, and Hall's illustrations.

And if the title needs explanation, here it is:

> I've gazed so much on beauty,
> it fills my vision to the brim.
>
> The body's contours. Red lips. Sensual limbs.
> Hair as if taken from Greek statues,
> always beautiful, even uncombed,
> and falling a bit against white foreheads.
> Faces of love, just as my poetry
> desired them ... in the nights of my youth,
> in my nights encountered secretly...

No sooner have I wished for more, than a new *Collected Poems* of Cavafy appears, from the poet Aliki Barnstone. The blurb boasts that she 'has been faithful to the original Greek, capturing both Cavafy's song and his vernacular in ways neglected in previous translations. Paying close attention to tone and diction, she has employed her poet's ear, making Cavafy's verse breathe new music in English.' My first impression was that these are indeed pretty smooth translations. But how do they compare with those of George Economou? Take a snip of Barnstone:

> Ah, now, there, now that he sits at the next table,
> I know each way he moves – and under his clothes,
> naked, are the loved limbs I see again.

Is this really English? Economou's version makes more sense and has more of a ring to it:

> Ah, there, now that he's sitting at the next table,
> I recognize every move he makes – and under his clothes
> I see again those beloved naked limbs.

No doubt it's unfair to compare versions like this, and there are plenty of places where all the translations of Cavafy are nearly word for word identical. Still, in his brief selection, Economou would seem to have the edge over Barnstone, and, indeed, over all the competition: he's sparkier, and punches harder.

Barnstone is determinedly pro-Greek (Selefkis, not Seleucus; Dareios not Darius) and she never lets us forget that Cleopatra is in fact Kleopatra. Sometimes her modernisms grate (kids, garbage, newlyweds), and she has dumped Cavafy's B.C. and A.D. in favour of B.C.E. and C.E. She is capable of writing things like, 'My whole being emanated/ pent-up sensual feeling' ['Outside the House'], and, 'Sometimes he earned his expenses/ for mediations considered shameful.' ['Days of 1896']. But if Barnstone has a few wonky moments, that is not to detract from her achievement in taking on (nearly) all of Cavafy. On the whole hers is a likeable version, smooth enough, maybe, with useful notes, and handsomely produced. It doesn't make the standard Keeley and Sherrard version redundant, nor does it replace Theoharis C. Theoharis's recent interesting edition, but it's worth a look.

Michael Kinsella

Nothing to Communicate, thankfully

Nick Laird, *To a Fault*, Faber, £8.99

Because our culture still tends to idealise poets, we might wonder what it would mean for a poet to think of himself as not being a persuasive user of words or as not having wondrous insights? *To a Fault* might be an answer to such a question. As a fascinated doubter of his own vocation, Nick Laird's case for poetry is defined by what it will not do. It is 'not a self-help guide ... // ... it's never enough for the mortgage' and neither is it 'memorable speech'. But through defining poetry by what it is not – it is not therapy, it is not financially rewarding and often utterly forgettable – Laird's anti-manifesto, 'Disclaimer', does give him an unusually assured sense of what poetry can be.

According to Laird, poetry is 'not lifting the pen from this page'. In other words, he seems to promote it as an act of will. It is also 'joined-up writing'. We might take that to mean that writing poems is about engaging with other literary predecessors. So, for instance, there are Joyceian, Frostian and Muldoonian mimickings distracting us as we read throughout this collection, and those voices seem to be there in order to purposefully flaw the potentially 'mesmeric' quality of Laird's verse. Like Muldoon, Laird seems absorbed by language but not seduced by it. Words are not to be trusted and nowhere is this more clearly and keenly felt than in the poems on his home.

Laird now lives in London, but he grew up around the market towns of Co.Tyrone in Northern Ireland. So, he's acutely aware, perhaps more than most, how words can create conflict. 'Cuttings', a lathery portrait of his 'angry and beautiful father' in a barbershop, reveals how local conversations about 'parking or calving or missing' are about not mentioning 'the troubles or women or prison.' Perhaps because of other responses to the violence (we might think here of poetry by Seamus Heaney, Derek Mahon or Michael Longley) or the post-ceasefire conditions, Ulster's troubles are fortunately not the most significant part of Laird's broader story. *To a Fault* has different backdrops – London's cityscape, 'The scaffolding clinging St. Paul's is less urban ivy than skin, peeling off', or modern Warsaw with its skyscrapers and capitalist awareness of brand names. But when sectarianism is recorded, 'The pistol jammed and they kicked him over./ They could break his legs, they offered,/ but he waited, and another gun was brought' ('The Signpost'), there is no moral indignation over the state of the nation. Instead, our staggering, even casual cruelty seems to be part of the larger comedy of being human. So in regard to the political and, it might be added, personal relationships, to filch a line from the book, Laird has 'nothing important to communicate', thankfully. There are no reassuring and consoling answers that try to make our predicaments go away. Yet neither is this poet a saboteur of human promise. Poems such as 'Aubade' and 'To The Wife' remind us, not only how ruthlessly but also how hopefully, we can love. As he says elsewhere, 'There is such a shelter in each other'. Writing *To a Fault* was perhaps Laird's way of establishing that potential, and a way of finding out if poetry was meant for him.

Alison Brackenbury

The shell

The empires fade. Villas in Spain,
Or Chedworth, crumble. Snails remain.

They sail and sway each broken wall,
No humble, thumb-sized snails that crawl

To fell your seedlings. These are huge,
Were brought to eat, be battered, chewed.

With shells translucent as dawn's floods
They slipped into the mossy woods

Missed fire and cries. Now safe, they rock
Down stony paths, until the fox

Noses their dens. Dim cream, nut-brown,
Forty rare shells lie tossed around.

The finest, violet-veined like blood
Is salvaged from the empty wood,

Washed of all trace of slime and self
Rolls up its kingdom, one bare shelf.

Solo

How can the oboe
Sing like a woman?
The long hair flows
Down the player's back.

How can he – yes, he -
Hold breath so long?
Young planets flee
The black horizon.

Dew gleams the long slopes
Of the park.
The notes fly fast
As bees from dark.

Wrap me in sleep
Toss down this care
A tumbled tune
A glistening hair.

Enclosed

I send you the wood
with its twist of path
the old carriage road,
time of slippery stones
of broken axles,
jolted bones.

I breathe you rough fruit
where the beech trees sail,
bunched oakleaves, torn
by the night's great gale.
In your mind, grown stiffly slow,
let this world's green tunnel flow.

Though you shake your head
as a horse flicks flies
no harm or ghost in the warmed leaf lies.
Do not linger in this wood
although west winds rise,
although rain beats hard
from your treeless skies.

Malcolm MacClancy

Réalta

I stand at the stable door, visiting you
Whose name means star.
If I was more still
The frost that has blanched the land
Would settle its icy grain on me too.
We blow at each other,
Our heads swathed In clouds of breath, both curious.
You move your hooves in the straw,
Shift your weight behind the half-door.
I turn away to the world of grey.
The lantern of a full-moon hangs
In the window of the windless night,
Its light spilt evenly over the country.
It is as if we are waiting for a sign,
Like a thief with his horse for company
In the back-yard of the galaxy.

Geraldine Paine

You were too young

He rides behind the coach and black-plumed four,
your sons and daughter ramrods by his side;
the horses' hooves he'd shod at six today,
farrier, husband, carrying on, astride
the racehorse you'd called *Storm* and tried to tame
by galloping through green cathedral lanes
that smelled of rain and badger setts and earth
disturbed by play. We stand, old friends and some
who simply knew your joy on days like these
before the winter dark undid the strings
of light. Behind the sunlit glass, a wreath
of trailing leaves becomes a forest floor
that hides you, still and shining girl, from sight.
We cry, you were too young. But so is he.

Linda Saunders

Dipper

How precisely the dipper
mimics these northern rivers,
darkness
being the most of him
but his bib white as their foam.

I've seen him dipdipping on a smooth rock
which divided the torrent
so it plumed and plunged with exactly
the sprung curve
    of his dive.

That dipdip now, and now,
timed to the fidget shadow-
    shine of the current,
like a repeated question.
Readiness? Impatience –
to be away or under,
each bob a feinted
    flight or dive?
Tic of attentiveness, intention –
to catch between
the slipping strata of the stream
    glimpse
of caddis larva, tiny fish.

Perhaps he must wind up resolution
    notch by notch –
to fly under water (truly
    he swims with his wings)
in a silver-lacquered glove of air
is no mean dynamic.

We watched him once, midwinter,
when the air was an aching grainy pastel,
ice seeded the earth,
    damasked the beck.

He was fishing from a bridge of ice
into a faster channel
which spread and gurgled underneath.
Can you remember?

A shadow-thought
questing behind a frosted mirror
before breaking into this world again
with the brown water
                            downstream.

Kelims in Stoke Newington

She's an ambassador spilling treasure
to kindle the languid gaze of princes,
or merchant who opens a bazaar of spices –
turmeric, black pepper, hot pimento.

Blue to quench parched eyes, pale gold
of quinces, pomegranates' absolute rose.
This one may be Russian – she brushes a palm
across the figured weave as one might appraise

the warm flank of a horse. *There were no more
made like this after 1927.*
You're lost in lore, maps vaguely enticing,
Balouch, Qashqai, mazes of encrypted prayer

while longed for groves and gardens are laid out on sand
to invite dreams of shadow, birdsong, flowers.
And you see a new geometry, not the static
balance of elements but nature's quick

reflections, echoes that give back changes
which the senses follow, questing, as light plays
over moving water, something like humour,
finding surprise and secrecy in the pattern.

You see how plane trees juggle the London summer
on their breezy leaves, to dance it through
the window across the kelims' blades and branches
and creamy lozenges of woven leaf-light.

Now she lifts and refolds, closing a distance
between outspread arms, strikes camp – and offers tea, as is the custom
in Turkey, to wash the wool dust from your throat.

Stuart Henson

The River at Rodmell

        I

At its end, the river draws
a salt transfusion,
the scum of the tideline
running the wrong way:
a brown gullet
backing up like a drain.
Only the poles of the cattle fence
go wading here, with a stave of weed-rags
dragged down between them.

You could pour
a whole lifetime away down this sluice
by the piles of the wharf
in the hum of the pylon lines.
And if there were some human thing
that cried to the sky in the blustering air
no-one would hear,
and the cattle would graze on unaware;
nor would the gulls care
as they loiter the length of the river's corridor
on their morning shift,
or sit out their watch
by the struts of the bridge
with their heads to the wind
in their neat white uniforms.

II

But each action, each step,
will alter the world forever.
You feed the blackbird
and later it blurts out the seed
of another orchard.
Your lunch, its carton,
the torn manuscript,
are all rolled round in the squall
whipped up from the landfill.

Pick out one stone,
weigh it and throw.
How can you know where the ripples end,
or the path of its slow eddying down
through a blind dimension?

If the train on its limited track
still goes hurrying past
you might wave,
and the face that waves back
will never be told
you weren't waving but changing

into that bent grey heron that broods like a stick
on the featureless shore.

Heather Coffey

Beating the Bounds

Each year when the hay is cut
the outline of The Rampin' Cat
surfaces from meadow grass,

echo of an alehouse,
the turf holding a memory
of sweat, the salt

which turned to rough house
after a few jars, downing
and spitting and swilling

until a man boxed his shadow
and wrestled with a wall.
And like a shadow it grows,

an image which doesn't last,
best seen from the sky
by crows and microlights

to vanish in later growth,
seamless and stricken,
as the rain pulls up

new grass, turning hay
into a few loose straws.
Unlike the contours of the well,

its slate tiled roof,
its freshly glossed permanence,
and undertow of women's voices,

a constant processional
to dip a pail for weddings
and funerals, golden traces

limping home in lives
which surface from the depths
in skeletons of leaves.

Tom MacIntyre

She

Unleavened bread leavens
my well-travelled tongue;
near the altar a spring;
votive redwood spade infers
the husbandry of breathing.

Here's the dunt of arrival,
here the heft of return,
here the vision candle,
here the gown ne'er torn...

You'll know my step, glance –
She departs for the fields,
mindful, Mother of The Plants,
Daughter of The Deep-Dish Leaves.

Scissors

For the visit, thank-you,
Lady. Prosperina, no doubt
you've heard, came by of late
(Royal Highness with daffodils),
Old Charon fingers his list,
my diet's roses and rue.

For your present, thank-you,
present, earnest, warrant,
the works. Ambience I salute,
uneven dirt-floor, lee
of the kitchen sink, no frills,
modest signature coup.

Wrap-up, Atropos, thank-you;
we take aboard the scissors'
mint complexion: ever in use,
snip-snip, snippety-snip,
they shine, Lady, your bladed
hansel, justly, shines as new.

Tania van Schalkwyk

My Grandmother's Art

'Quand je vois la Vie en Rose'- Edith Piaf

My grandmother would paint my face
in imaginary colours with her fingertips
gently caress beauty and belonging into me.
As we lay on an afternoon bed resting from the tropical heat
she explained each brush stroke of her imagination:
And now I am painting in your lips ... the colour is exquisite ... the
curve of your brow magnificent –
you are like a wild rare orchid.
Her words were filled with flourish, exaggerated by love.
She made my face feel like it belonged beautifully in the world.
I continue to paint my face now her hands are gone –
only mine are not always gentle, hued in love –
sometimes nails scratch cheeks red as blood is bit from lips,
other times, I retrace the portrait of my grandmother's flower –
and I tint my scarred eyes in rose water – disguise the etchings with
bold strokes of hope and remembrance across the canvas that is my skin.

Viv Apple

Father Figure

Then you,
hammering my resentment
into the ground,
forgot how small I was.
I learned to watch that look,
staring down and bleak
before a hand stung my leg –
my lesson when you came home tired
and couldn't stand a noise.
That would stop it
stoppit, stoppit, stop!

so I stopped
making decisions;
biting my fingers;
answering back.
Being.

Became your decisions.
Asked no questions.
Silently
watching your jawline
for that tell-tale clench.

Quietly,
I peeped out of the Sunday boredom
onto the street where hopscotch hollers
were forbidden music,
sweet as wild chives
chewed from beside the railway track.

Now
in this old photograph,
all I can see from your slight smile
and well-intentioned eyes
is love.

Perhaps you tried hiding the scars
of your own dark Sundays.
It's not your fault
that you could not translate
the way you meant to be,
before you died.

Mark Leech

The Beast

Cornersniffer, with the hooked rasp of an old man
pissing in the hedge.
                            Your hand
all sweat on the back door latch
      but when you get to where you thought you heard –
         just a few hard leaves
         spinning like miraculous dishes
         in your neighbour's kitchen light.

He treads softly
in hibernation season:
your windows
              flicker with his passing,
rainwater shudders free as he slips
under the laurel   over the lawn.

One night he'll be between you
and the house
              an eye flashed for your breath-winged heart.

Your thoughts lurch desperate for the hallway warm
with your belongings –
              his clawed strength slashes
the skin of memory
              and you're blinking
in an empty garden   your home open, bright.

Judith Kazantzis

In Rome

My dear, you renew your life too often...
Te qui odi et amo...

When you are ill
      the great halls of tapestry
remember themselves quickly as bland, expert
with the muscled bodies of that trance,
      silent and sensuous, by torture
at the fingers of white-muscled executioners,

and they rifle the metal hall of night,
and they sight the slow golden morning.

Autumn is here. Don't the men sit still and write
      of the plough and the earth,
of country women with the fruitful, high-held baskets.
Let us praise the poets and their conventions.

When you are well
      the voluminous apricot folds
of the laundered skirts and the crisp transparent fichu, the new turban of
the sybil, or any woman you may like

better, sailing on the Sistine ceiling, conferring
      as fresh as a practical woman,
a prospering merchant of some ways and means,
brings back the success of fruit and peaceful light:
      considerate, clever,
conversation cocked to her neighbour.

No gilded lily, but given over to your fate,
comfortable, conscious of the sun

sufficient, gold for today. In her fold pocket
      there hugs a death by air
and such racks, and then all the glorious what ifs -
well buried, like a hoop of house-keys,
      in her voluminous apricot apron...

Marc Harris

A Century of Sounds: The Fork

(To my grandfather who was in the medical corps during World War I. At 16, having lied about his age, he became a stretcher-bearer at the battle of Mons. After the war, when in the Merchant Navy, the fork he used to eat with in the trenches went with him on his world travels and is in my mother's hands to this day.)

It rings when struck –
grandfather's fork.
With J.P.J.
John Penry Jones
engraved on its handle;
cutlery
from the trenches,
Mons, Ypres, Flanders Fields;
hands that held it,
sensitive
to screams,
shells and men.

Then in merchantmen,
it fathomed the pitch of waves,
crashed
against the thin skin of the hull,
tuned choirs of gulls,
dolphins' song.

In the carnivals of Rio,
rich tones of a Suez seaport
honed its silver sheen.

Now
sounds of a century sing
for Johnny
of the Bluebell Inn,
Ceinewydd,
Ceredigion.

Pneumoconiosis

(Black lung disease)

In intricate ways
the black dust
had mapped out his life.

In the bronchioles,
alveoli of his lungs,
seams of coal had settled.

He mined mucous now,
this small, shrivelled man
from Ynysybwl –
coughing up his guts
on cold, dark days in Wales.

Compensation took him to China
where he met the Terracotta Army;
walked the Great Wall
as far as he could
on the strongest of steroids –
three inhalers to hand.

Over a bitter
we talked.

After all,
his surgeon had said,

'Enjoy yourself'.

Richard Marggraf Turley

Afterlives

I

Blink

'Languille!'*

The guillotined eyes
open like an oiled
machine, then sag
and seal.

'Languille!'

The dead hood
remembers. Just
eyes. See.

'Languille!'

Glaze.

II

Queen of Scots†

'Dogs will lick her blood' (John Knox)

*Never undressed
before such company.*

We fixed a cloth to her
caul. It was the white neck
she wished to screen.
After the blood her skirts
trembled, the crowd
pushed and groaned. We pulled off her garters:
there was Geddon for love
under her petticoats.

---

* Convicted murderer, executed 1905
† Mary took her Skye terrier with her to execution, 1587

III

News from the Dead*

Good friends –
jigging up dead
weight and jerking
down hard with love
to speed the rope,
thumping the
breast till breath-
less in hope of still-
ing that awkward
pulse.
        I came to
under the dissector's
knife. Then poultices,
clysters, rub.

Debouching

Some ways to break
cover. Girard's steady river
spilled from the stones
at Saint Amand –

splashed the fog saddle
jib of gun sprung-
blinking crawling in
furnaces o the
small mouths –

all facing that bright
fluid instant.

---

* Anne Greene, accused of infanticide, was executed in 1650. She was resuscitated by the surgeon who collected her 'corpse' for medical purposes. The title is that of the 1651 pamphlet relating the 'miracle'.

Matthew Geden

Ghosts

We are not as revolutionary as before
when we slipped out of the material
world and into the shadows where love
is a permanent affair. We've lived
lives of smoke fuelled by the idea
of fire; the warmth of confidential kisses
sustained us through the dark and we
designed dreams, an intimate manifesto.
Somehow, now, the world is colder frosted
breath a presence in the air where
echoes fall like snow in Highgate
cemetery. We have endured, committed
ourselves to substance; watching the dawn-
grey light chipping away at the headstones.

Gracious Networks

(after Li Ho)

seated on the terrace
as the stars plummet
into the darkening pool

an unidentified figure
sips from a glass
mid-life slips away

migrant birds proclaim
change hibiscus blossoms
bleed into the soil

long neglect lies ahead
but certain words
never quite forgotten.

Sally Lucas

The Recitation

Through other people's notes,
A rise of phrase
Or scent that floats
Unhurried out of the near face

Splashing sound, we follow
Trails of hand
From mouth to brow
Rapt: though may not understand

What it is we taste
In a line's swell
Cresting without haste,
And we may not tell

What shines bright in eyes
Over the lips' cave
But will try to prise
Meaning from each breath's wave

Hush of swallows
Into the dark,
Craving the stark
Words' blissful hollows.

Lisa Dart

Annunciation

*Zachariah is visited by an angel who says,
though both he and his wife are old, they will have a child
to be called John. Because Zachariah doubts, he is made
dumb until the birth of the child. Luke 1 (5–63)*

Nine mute months
pass in disbelief.
Zachariah stares, nightly, at the sky –

ordinary portent of God. No aurora
borealis of angel, gold, tower of radiance,
harbinger of birth

or other glad tidings. Unlike that time
at the temple where he, prostrate skeptic
in priest's robes, insists:

But I am old ... Amid light, wings,
prophecy, the angel speaks: *Behold
thou shalt be dumb,
until that day these things shall be performed.*

He has not uttered since. His hand
ineffable, articulates
the final swelling of her belly –
Elisabeth's time imminent –
until Zachariah

cradles, bloody moment born, a son.
Scrawls a name. Stammers. Cries out
to a starry wilderness. Nascent. Guttural –

the stars echo John ... John ... John.

Chosen Young Broadsheet Poet: Simon Pomery

Anima

The wing of a crow lay
on the stone grate
by the fire,
burnt off an unlucky nester.

Even the white of a swan's wing
(used here as a feather-duster
to rake soot with a dustpan) could not poke it free
and startle the live jizz of a bird back into sky.

Each black feather
pointed to an ember
as the smoulder
lessened, hung in a shopping basket of flames

flicking the feathers' shadows
on the stone,
as though the image might
animate a flash of alula.

Uncle Rodge

When he fell, no, when he *dropped*
out of his life, in a flash
they put to his lips a morphine lollypop–
cubic and blue as that swill of mouthwash

I spat in a Wicklow sink the day of his burial,
acting on advice to clean the wisdom teeth
swelling in my mouth. Meanwhile
my jaw locked with *trismus*, leaving me speechless.

The Folksinger

When the streetlamp flickered on her face,
her hair was the colour of terracotta.
I thought of horses off the Atlantic track
past Moran's Oyster Cottage;

of the man who stripped off and swam across the Weir,
from Moran's to his own horse. He lost
hold of the rein more than once
as he yanked and yawped to make it wade.

And as it dried, I thought of the ivy-pot
that split and leaked its roots over the stone,
the pot we put out in the courtyard, cracked
from watering it a day before the frost.

The house belonging to the court is clear
of our belongings. She and I lost touch.
I think it was the swimmer who waved his torch
on us that night, its beam across *my* face.

Beside the Weir, she sang to me one song
from every city on her gap-year route–
Sarajevo, Tunis, Barcelona.
I gave, in return, one kiss for each place.

By morning, she was gone. My uncle Rodge
had *passed away in the night*. I'd like to think
that by such contraries the memory
is constituted, casketed, and locked.

Send No Flowers

Send no Polianthes,
and certainly not the two
purpling daisies burst
through

so early in their bed
of nothing
else
but sown bulbs, having

come even earlier
than those violet crocuses
held by the blonde girl

in a mock funeral–
her dress Venus Looking Glasses,
her song of a lost pearl.

Notes for Broadsheet Poets 7

As stated earlier in this series, all poets, young and old, need some kind of a mentor, whether living or dead, whether a teacher, listener, or critical appreciator.

Gerard Smyth, the Irish poet whose latest collections have been published by Dedalus Press, writes movingly about the kind of mentor we all need. This elegy, then, brings back to life an important mentor from his youth, a school-teacher who invoked other mentors no longer living, and whose inspiration caused 'the riddles and orisons' of his pupils to 'rise from the page'.

Riddles and Orisons

To the memory of Jack Hoey, teacher

Straight-backed, arms outflung,
in front of everyone
he stood like a singer about to sing
his favourite aria.
The dust of school-chalk
lay on his shoulders.

He read with both eyes closed,
brooded over Matthew Arnold
and Samuel Coleridge
during the last lesson of the day
when in a voice that was ceremonious
he created the atmosphere of the Lakes
just by saying *Windermere*.

Shakespeare, Yeats,
Father Hopkins, Soldier Ledwidge.
On afternoons when the glinting sun
came in or rain fell hard
on the window-ledge
he made their riddles and orisons
rise from the page.

Peter Abbs, poet and Professor of Creative Writing at the University of Sussex, addresses all poets, from his wide experience, in the following essay and invokes mentors who are well-known poets from both the past and the present:

The Four Tasks of the Contemporary Poet

What marks the work of the poet and how does it relate to our new twenty-first century? Out of a number of contending possibilities I will select what I see as four key elements of the poet's creative engagement and, as I move forward, endeavour to relate them to our times.

The existential dimension

I believe the work of the poet should be existentially grounded. Being a poet is an interior vocation, not a selected career. A poem is a highly personal opening of experience which could not have been written by anyone else, not quite in that way, with that cadence, that image, that peculiar specificity of language. Emily Dickinson represents, superbly, this aspect of the poet's work as individual, almost idiosyncratic, perception and interpretation, however precarious:

I stepped from Plank to Plank
A slow and cautious way
The Stars about my Head I felt
About my Feet the Sea.

I knew but not the next
Would be my final inch –
This gave me that precarious Gait
Some call Experience.[1]

The word 'experience' in this poem denotes an obfuscating abstraction hiding the appalling varieties of individual life which it is the poet's exacting work not only to map, but also to incarnate in language, to make available to our collective imaginative life. For Emily Dickinson to be, to exist (ex – sistere), *to stand out,* is to step diffidently into a cosmic immensity that involves the imminent possibility of death.

The work is to find one's own voice, the voice which utters precisely the individuality of vision – or if not vision, dislocation, disjuncture, disorientation – giving it cognitive shape and expressive form. In the broadest sense it is an educational labour. The struggle – always restless and forever incomplete – is to recognize, often through the act of writing, in the frustrating tussle with language, the nature of the feeling, the nature of the sensation, the nature of the state of consciousness. It demands a remarkable authenticity of being. T.S Eliot called the English poet William Blake 'a man born without a mask'. For there are times when one would rather not know one's own thoughts and feelings, when one would rather adopt a mask, seek refuge in the collective banalities of the age, in the easy distractions of counterfeit comfort, in what Heidegger called *das Man.*[2]

Part of the exacting work of the poet is to annihilate the mind's protective defences and to silence the seductive voices of what others would like to hear, the clamorous expectations of the zeitgeist.

There is a story told by the Danish philosopher, Kierkegaard, of a doctor who has just lost his loved one. In a state of grief verging on dementia, he wanders out of his town and comes to a small hamlet. There the doctor goes into the church and finds himself seeking consolation from the minister. The minister listens and is full of compassion. However, he finally admits he cannot help but claims he knows of a book which many of his parishioners, in a state of acute mourning, have found an invaluable support. He takes a volume off the shelf and holds it out to the stricken doctor. The man stares at it, disbelievingly, and says; 'Ah, no. That will not help. You see, I myself am the author.'

For writers this is an uncomfortable story. I am wanting to see writing as an existential labour and am implying an inexpungeable subjective element in all significant creation. Unlike the doctor's book on mourning, there should be a living – if highly complex and often refracted – connection between the person writing and the poem written, between the author struggling and the artefact made. This position sharply contrasts with T.S. Eliot's; in *Tradition and The Individual Talent* Eliot claimed that 'the progress of an artist is a continual self-sacrifice, a continual extinction of personality'.[3] I think this is neither possible, nor desirable. The very idiom of the artistic work retains the unique impress of its creator. (That is why in the visual arts we talk of a *Picasso,* a *Chagall,* a *Rembrandt,* and why most conceptual art fails to convince and seems utterly soulless, literally machine-made, machine-fabricated.) In the work of Emily Dickinson *her* unmistakeable idiom is marked by the telegrammatic line, the erratic use of capitals, quirky use of the hyphen, extreme verbal condensation and the all but breathless brevity of the utterance.

A fine modern example of this existential element in poetry would be Ted Hughes' 'Wodwo', a poem which, written in Hughes' intense and graphic idiom, begins with the question 'What am I?' and continues exploring the radical uncertainties of this animal – 'I seem / separate from the ground and not rooted but dropped/ out of nothing casually' ... Hughes concludes:

...I am the exact centre
but there's all this what is it roots
roots roots roots and here's the water
again very queer but I'll go on looking[4]

Above all, Wodwo is a dazed animal caught in some elemental quest, a symbolic representation of the author's being.

The linguistic dimension

So poetry should be existentially grounded, possess the quality of a compelling personal integrity. But the poet must also be deeply aware of the medium in which he or she works: language. I see this as the second element of the poetic engagement. All good poets are naive philologists in the original sense of that word – they are *lovers of words*. One recalls John Keats who, even as a child, had such a creative and playful relationship to language. A Mrs Grafty claimed that as a small boy instead of answering questions put to him, he would always make up a rhyme to resonate with the last word spoken, laughing with pleasure as he did so. And then in the last anguished months of his short life he brought the same verbal playfulness to hold back the ordeal of suffering, so as not to be a burden on others: summoning up, as he said, 'more puns in a sort of desperation in one week than in any year of my life'.[5]

Poets are the votaries of language. They are in love with its music, its multiple significations, its etymologies.

Now language is informed by, at least, three distinct functions:

Denotation
Connotation
Cadence

As poetry is language, animated to the highest degree, it follows that poetry must integrate these three powers to the greatest possible intensity in relationship to the purpose of the poem. The work of the poet is to drive all three elements into a single compelling constellation. Adapting a magnificent line from Gerard Manley Hopkins I would suggest that 'the significant poem is charged with the grandeur of language'.

Inevitably, many poems fail this high synthesis: they may denote without cadence (too many poems, these days, seem little more than moralistic or political tags written on the page in broken lines of prose; politically correct tags as heavy as lead) or they connote without meaning (like, it seems to me, some of Dylan Thomas' poems that are diffusely suggestive but seem to be entirely devoid of cognitive significance) or they have cadence without sense (like kinetic poetry, now currently enjoying a certain vogue).

Of course, much critical analysis could be done here. But my general point is simple. The poet has to truly love the language out of which poems are made. A poem is not an encoded message, nor is it an idea set to metre. It is a unique linguistic creation. It calls for a pitched, almost painful, sensitivity to the potencies of syntax, concept, association, metaphor and cadence. Yet there is a dilemma here. Can we really talk about 'the grandeur of language' in our times when, for a multiplicity of interacting reasons, the language is so exhausted, so polluted, when all affirmation sounds only like advertising hyperbole? Indeed is poetry, in the way I have described it, possible today? Can it be written? Perhaps to ask for grandeur is to ask too much?

Here, I think, we can learn from the poet Paul Celan who worked to cleanse the German language from the toxins left by Fascism. In his difficult, labyrinthine, musical poems he all but decomposed and reconstituted the German language in order to express his own nuances, his existential meanings, his own profoundly oppositional understanding. In his poems the distortion of conventional syntax, the employment of gaps, the brevity, the occlusions and the silences (his idiom has a certain affinity with Emily Dickinson's whose work he translated into German) are frayed attempts to utter what the dominant language had made all but unsayable.

In one of his speeches Paul Celan said:

> Only one thing remained reachable, close and secure amid all losses: language. Yes, language. In spite of everything, it remained secure against loss. But it had to go through its own lack of answers, through terrifying silence, through the thousand darknesses of murderous speech. It went through. It gave me no words for what was happening but went through it. Went through and could resurface, 'enriched' by it all.[6]

The word 'enriched' *is* the affirmative word. The following poem is a personal attempt to express in English something of what I think Celan is doing. (For a more literal translation of the poem 'Psalm' and for the original poem in German the reader should consult *Paul Celan: Selected Poems* edited by Michael Hamburger.)

Psalm

No-one can create us again out of the dust.
No-one.

Never.

Hallowed be thy name, No-one.
Who is not in Heaven.

Not the Power.

Nor the Glory.

For your sake
We live and flower.

We are not roses –
Our stamens broken,
Our stems blood red.

Not in the beginning.

Nor in the end.

Flowering now and for never,
Without

Amen.[7]

   I think contemporary poets may be able to learn from the example of Celan. For today's corrupt language can be undermined, taken down into unexpected depths, washed in the darkness and brought to a kind of grandeur that transcends. And, no doubt, any such grandeur will, at times, sound disconcertingly ambiguous for it will have to be an 'enrichment' which, like Celan's, has taken into its own form the terror of absolute negation and the power of silence.
   In spite of all appearances, the task of writing poetry has never been more in question, more difficult, more at the edge.

The cultural dimension

The third element of the poet's work relates to seeing the task as collaborative, of feeling that there *is* a long tradition to be read and raided, to be taken forward *in extremis*. In the present state of cultural dissipation an inner connection to a larger symbolic world is essential for the imaginative life. It is no accident that Ted Hughes' animal Wodwo is taken from *Sir Gawain and the Green Knight* or that the source of Celan's poem is biblical.

However, tradition is far too stolid and stable a word for what I mean; I would rather talk about *the dynamic field in which literature lives.* In a recent book *Against the Flow*[8] I put the general case like this:

Any real poetics in Europe – and that is where we live – must be mapped inside a remarkable culture that goes back and back; from T.S.Eliot and Paul Celan and Mandelstam, through Coleridge and Goethe, through Shakespeare and Dante to Ovid, Sappho and Homer – and the shamans and myth-makers before them. There can be no escaping the tradition for, again and again, an individual word will carry ancient poetic sediment and one of the poet's tasks – as language is the poet's medium – is to shake the hidden pollen and seeds that lie there, to allow for a new and quite unexpected fertilisation. An endless linguistic resurrection! Not to work the deep geology of language is to fail the medium.

We should envisage Sappho, Dante, Shakespeare and Dickinson as our corrective contemporaries. This frees us, at once, from the blinding oppression of fashion and the jangle of journalistic tags. Keeping such good company also constantly challenges our range.

Paradoxically, such a 'tradition' can offer a means to get closer to the raw feel of contemporary experience, without sounding glib or merely rhetorical. The works of the past provide a repertoire of protagonists and narratives which may allow the poet to view *imaginatively* the betrayals and the brute violence of our times. Michael Longley in his celebrated poem 'Ceasefire' by employing Homer's account of the meeting of Hector and Achilles in *The Iliad* is able the more effectively to broach the sectarian violence in Northern Ireland. In this poem Homer's narrative offers a distancing frame for the moving contemplation of contemporary suffering.

In a similar manner I adapted the opening of Canto Three from Dante's *Inferno* to try to capture what I saw as the cultural barbarism of the time, in 1992:

Dante to Virgil at the Entrance to Hell

And so we came to that place unrecorded in books
Or maps; not found in archives or libraries.
The night smouldered without stars. At times
It was so dark I could see nothing. On all sides
There rose gagged screams, muffled sighs;
A mixture of filth, insinuation, jargon, lies.
Be economical with the truth, one says. Another cries:
Humanity, what is that? Tears pricked my eyes.
And all the time a blizzard scoured the place;
A million grains of sand blistered my face.
Master, I said, *For Christ's sake who are these men?*
The answer came at once. *They are the nation's scum,
Which rises quickly. They are maggots that worm
Their way through venison. Survivors, to the end;
Who learning the art of words become the masters of deceit;
Yet are always silent when it serves them well.
Observe them closely. For we are at the entrance into hell.*
It was then I saw that banner whipping the wind,
Zig-zagging as it swirled, now *Left,* now *Right,*
Now *Low,* now *High.* Such a mob followed on –
Who would have thought death had undone so many?
From their blotched faces blood streamed to the ground
Where bloated worms rose up, to gulp it down.[9]

The poem, like Michael Longley's, is a form of re-telling, a way of putting the great literary work of the past to new uses. It is, of course, only one obvious way in which the contemporary poet can work the field of literature. In fact, the influence of other historic work is *always* there, often in the most subtle way, beating in the syntax, adding another layer of meaning to a metaphor or further animating a particular word.

That the voices of this literary tradition are growing fainter each day in our technocratic global culture poses a real problem for the poet. This, indeed, lies at the heart of the current crisis of poetry. But without this vast echo-chamber of multiple cadence, resonant with the verbal creation of centuries, there can be no significant poetry – only a one-dimensional whittering.

The metaphysical dimension

I have often thought that the real value of art is that it creates embodied representations of life for our contemplation, both for our aesthetic pleasure and our inner renewal. We should not, in an age of unparalleled trivia and vaunted mediocrity, give up on this vivifying notion. If we yield the high ground, what have we left: an empty formalism, entertainment, verbal quips for passing occasions, Polonius-like platitudes, the seductions of advertising? To concede here is to compose our epitaph.

In the 'Ninth Elegy' of the *Duino Elegies* Rilke wrote:

Now is the time for telling, *here* is the place.
Speak and testify. More than ever
those things we have lived with are falling away...
but our hearts fight back, living
between the hammers, and our tongues
sing on between our teeth, in spite
of everything, singing and praising.[10]

Poets have little choice but to live between the menacing hammers, still labouring to utter the multiform truths of our being *here*, of our being *now*, thus keeping open through the power of language and the continuous resurrection of 'tradition' the creative possibilities of consciousness. This I would name the metaphysical task of poetry.

The word 'metaphysical' can easily be misunderstood. I do not use the word to refer to a body of supernatural truths which can be scanned through the power of reason, but rather to describe our predicament as human beings; through our powers of symbolising we lift ourselves out of nature and become enigmas to ourselves. The metaphysical begins with this dilemma: who are we? how do we belong? what can we create out of our puzzling natures? The question that Wodwo asks is the perennial metaphysical question: what am I? And the answer that he gives is in no way doctrinal but a matter of orientation: *I'll go on looking*. Nothing is certain in this realm, but everything in our lives may rest on the answers we hazard. In my view, significant poetry has to grapple with this huge question of meaning or, rather, *the possibility of meaning*. At times it amounts to no more than the task of witnessing what seems absent. In the following poem from my recent volume, *Viva la Vida,* the fox carries the projection of the missing god.

Red Fox

What were we looking for? Each morning as the train raced
Between urban stations – disused, vandalized – we watched
The fields glide by. Patches of chemical green, withered marsh,

Scarred land. From the window we scanned the margins,
Impatient to claim whatever stricken life ran at the edges –
To catch the red fox sprinting reckless under spiked iron ledges,

Its tail scorching tinder ground. And momentarily we caught him
In his new habitat, loping by a scree of cars, a metal mound,
A smouldering stream or suspended between action, his green eyes

Staring, his paws reading the raw braille of the broken earth.
Gone almost before seen – like a sudden image come to birth
In a deep-sleep dream ... *Fox! Fox!* We shouted – only to witness

The trauma of his absence. But his rank beauty entered us,
Taunted our tamed hours, haunted us like a god – lost
In that corroded hinterland. Yet radiant still. *Deus absconditus.*[11]

Poetry's task is to burn, blow and make us new. But also, at times, to perplex and unsettle us, to keep us unstable and open to change. In both roles, positive and negative, it is the arch-enemy of the one dimensional consumer society we now inhabit.

Notes and references

1 *The Complete Poems of Emily Dickinson* (1957) ed Thomas Johnson, New York, Little Brown and Company.
2 *Das Man.* This is Heidegger's coinage meaning, literally, the 'one' or the 'they'; the one who does what 'one' should do, the one who conforms, the 'they-self'.
3 See *Selected Prose of T.S.Eliot* (1975) ed. Frank Kermode, Faber and Faber.
4 'Wodwo' is the concluding poem in *Wodwo* (1967), Ted Hughes, Faber and Faber.
5 Both these details concerning Keats' life are recorded in *John Keats: a Life* (1995), Stephen Coote, Hodder and Stoughton.
6 See *Paul Celan: Collected Prose* (1999), translated by Rosmarie Waldrop, Carcanet.
7 *Personae and Other Selected Poems* (1995), Peter Abbs, Skoob Books
8 *Against the Flow: Education, the Arts and Postmodern Culture* (2003), Peter Abbs, RoutledgeFalmer.
9 Op cit.
10 From *The Duino Elegies,* Rainer Maria Rilke translated by Leslie Norris and Alan Keele (1993), Camden House.
11 From *Viva la Vida* (2005), Peter Abbs, Salt. www.saltpublishing.com

Songs and Dreams as Sources of Poetry

This next piece is about how inspiration and the creative process of writing a poem works. It is written by **Steven O'Brien**, a poet of Irish/Welsh origins, brought up in Sussex, whose first collection, ***Dark Hill Dreams***, much admired by Irish Poet, Brendan Kennelly, was published this year by ***Agenda Editions*** (£8.99. Order from The Wheelwrights, Fletching Street, Mayfield, East Sussex TN20 6TL, tel. 01435 873703, or by email: editor@agendapoetry.co.uk)

Poetry advances where ordinary reality falters
        (Bachelard, On Poetic Imagination and Reverie)

Many Irish songs and stories speak of the ragged outcast Rapparee: a fallen nobleman of the Gaelic aristocracy, turned outlaw. The beginning of my poem called 'I Sing the Rapparee' goes as follows:

In the eyes-closed ache of the song
He jags in my vision,
Sudden against the skyline.
Hounded youth –
The Rapparee.

I catch the shattered cut of him
As he hares across
The crow-mobbed sodden hillside of the tune.
Russet jacket rags
Flap and part
To show a winter thicket of ribs
And a shot-out heart.

This one image lies at the core of my poem: the hunted man with the shot out heart. I experienced this as a waking dream. I had been wrestling with ideas for poems. I sat through most of Sunday writing lines and not getting anywhere with them. I had no subject, or central idea in my mind. I was teaching full-time and Sundays were the only time I could devote to writing. I went to bed late, knowing that I had to be up early in the morning.

    I dreamed of a man scurrying and running in light rain across a near vertical, green mountainside. He was wearing a tattered jacket, and he had black, wet hair. He seemed to be about thirty. At one point, almost as if I had zoomed in to him, in a cinematographic shot, I was suddenly very close to him. I found myself looking up at him, from a position of about three feet lower down the steep slope. He stopped still for an instant, although his chest was heaving from much running. He did not look at me and did not appear to be aware of my presence. As his jacket parted in the wind, I looked at his chest and stomach. I saw that, instead of ribs, his frame was made of wicker-work, like the underside of a woven basket. It was also like looking through a copse thicket, or wintry hedge, as there were dry leaves clinging to the twigs. However there was a shattered hole in the centre of his chest and I knew that this man had been shot. I saw that there was an empty space where his heart should be. I could catch glimpses of the back of his jacket through the tangle. I knew, in the sudden, emphatic way knowledge comes in a dream, that this man was at the same time both alive and dead.

In the instant of his halting I was aware only of his tall, thin image, the wind like fluttering ribbons and the creaking of his wicker-thicket ribcage, as he gasped for breath. He turned his head and ran up the mountain to the ridge. I saw in his eyes a last expression of desperate panic, as he scanned the horizon. Then he was gone. Then I heard, far off, the baying of many hounds coming unseen from over the peaks behind me. Suddenly I, too, was running and filled with fear. I ran up the mountain, just as the man had done, and on to a rock-strewn plateau. But he was gone and I did not see him again.

Now I had the feeling that the pack was after me and that I had to escape at all costs. It became one of those terrible dream sequences when one runs and runs, but it is never fast or far enough to escape the pursuers. Finally, I climbed over broken walls and hid in the ruins of a tumbled stone house. I too was now gasping for breath and wet through with rain and sweat. I looked out from behind the chimney stack to see the hounds throng through a gap in the low wall. They did not seem to notice me. Instead they took a scent and their cries pitched around the stones, as they poured straight past where I was hiding. I knew that they were chasing the man with the shot-out heart. There were no human pursuers. I was left looking out over the green plateau through gaps in the grey walls. And there the dream ended.

I awoke and knew instantly that I had been dreaming of the Rapparee. There was no doubt about it in my mind. I knew enough songs and stories to piece together that my dream of flight and pursuit had been about the hunted Irish outlaw. It was one of those intense and complex dreams that stay with one long into waking.

In *On Poetic Imagination and Reverie*, Bachelard states, 'The image-producing forces of our mind develop along two very different lines. The first take wing when confronted by the new. The other forces which produce images plumb the depths of being. There they seek at once the primitive and eternal'.

The new forces which produced the images of setting in the poem were immediately apparent to me. I had recently returned from a visit to my wife's family home in County Limerick. I recognised the mountainside in my dream, from a walk we took, one day in the rain, with my wife's cousin. There is a steep slope and summit called Barna, which forms the beginning of the uplands of Limerick. The setting of my dream was the top of Barna, or a place just like it. On our walk along the plateau we were shown the ruins of cottages vacated in the famine of the 1840s. There were a tumble of grey stones, grassy mounds and a few upstanding structures, which were explained as the ruins of chimneys. These are the 'strewn walls' of my poem.

Sullen black cattle stood, blank-eyed, and still in the desolation, as shifts of rain drifted across the remnants. The cottages looked to have been very small, tiny even. I stood in the gap and touched both empty spaces where walls would have stood. We spoke of the hard lives of subsistence, parcels of divided land, and large families in cramped cabins. The endless mean struggle, with only buttermilk and potatoes to eat, and when the potato failed, nothing.

Nothing but *An Górta Mór* – The Great Hunger.

On the way down, against the wind and rain, we spoke of the famine, telling over again stories that had been passed down to us, through the conduit of generations. Sharp flints of suffering, worked by tongues, into smooth, commonly held stones. We spoke of mass evictions, and the roof thatch torched by the landlords' men. Of the corn, gold and ripe, in the landlords' fields and mothers lying in ditches, their mouths stained green, from eating grass. Of dead babies at their dry breasts. Of glutted crows over broken fields. Of skeletal men walking the land, beyond hope, until they fell. Of a million dead, and two million fled across the wide ocean. And the ruins we had left behind on Barna seemed to serve as an equinoctial point for the familiar currency we shared. I remember I found myself singing lines from the old song 'Skibbereen':

> Oh father dear and I often hear
> You speak of Erin's isle
> Her valleys green her lofty scenes
> Her mountains rude and wild
> They say it is a lovely land
> In which a prince might dwell
> Then why did you abandon it
> The reason to me tell...

Below Barna, at the home of my wife's uncle, we were shown a massive and twisted old oak tree on the roadside, which is known locally as the *'Hanging Tree'*, its large bough having been used for public executions in the penal days. On another uncle's farm we were told how he had found two skeletons while he was digging out an old sand-pit. The remains were sent to Dublin and the results of the tests revealed them to have been of a mother and teenage daughter, both victims of the famine.

I remember sitting quietly in the old cottage that night. My wife and I listened to the rain pelting the windows. I thought of the stories of the famine and old songs of rebels; the broken houses, and a few wet fields away, the two lonely graves. I thought too of Liam O Maonlaí's mournful singing of Peatsi O'Callanán's lament *White Potatoes*, which dates from the time of the Hunger;

> *A thousand farewells to the white potatoes*
> *For as long as we had them, a pleasant hoard*
> *Affable innocent, coming into our company*
> *As they laughed at the head of the board.*
>
> *They were help to the nurse, to the man and the child,*
> *To the weak and the strong, to the young and the old*
> *But the cause of my sorrow, my grief, my affliction*
> *Them rolling away, without frost, without cold.*
>
> *What will buy a shroud for those to be buried?*
> *Tobacco, pipes or a coffin of wood?*
> *And, of course, it would be a release if we could.*

I went and stood in the open doorway and looked into the blackness, thinking of the shivering Rapparee, tattered, and soaked., crouching under tumbled stones, gnawing a putrid potato. His cutlass blunt, his shelmalier musket a rusty relic. This all occurred weeks before my dream. Now when I consider Bachelard's thoughts on the image-producing forces, I am minded of the assault of the past on the present that occurred in my few days in Limerick. In 'Stations of the West', Heaney writes, 'all around me seemed to prophesy'. In those days, I too felt the landscape and the past prophesying vividly to me. And although there was no immediate poetry, my mind must have been primed by all that I had seen or heard around Barna. However, unlike Heaney and his rootedness, my journey into Irish culture has always been through the myths at the heart of old songs, and as the poem first began to lodge itself on that Monday morning, it was the fabulous and harsh mythic elements of the dream which fired my imagination the most. To me, this is what Bachelard intends when he comments on the 'primitive and eternal'.

Before breakfast and work, I wrote some lines down in a fast and rough way. The lines I sketched were those which reflected the most disturbing part of the dream: the central, perplexingly surreal image of a man, at once alive and dead, with a cage of twigs for ribs. They have been revised slightly, but they still perform as the imaginative kindling at the core of the finished poem

>   Russet jacket rags
>
>   Flap and part
>
>   To show a winter thicket of ribs
>   And a shot-out heart.

These lines have changed very little from those I wrote on the first morning of the poem's inception. 'Russet' was a word added in a later draft. The fact remains that whatever the poem's strengths may be, for me, the poem arose from this vivid, shocking dream. The wider implications of the dream on my poetry were a long time coalescing. However, I have come to see the poem as both the beacon from which all the poetry I have written over the last six years emanates, and also the magnet to which many of my images are held by attractive force.

Thus 'I Sing the Rapparee' contains themes which evolve and manifest themselves in later poems. Enchantment figures are an ingredient in the most intense of my poems. Strong archetypal figures surface in poems about my mother, my sister, the Guy Fawkes group and the poems concerning the Prophet. They are all outsiders, strangers, hunted. To employ an Old Saxon term – they are all held under some terrible wyrd. A famished anomie burns in their restless eyes.

Linked to this is the violence of many of my poems, with recurrent ideas of sacrifice, brutality and martyrdom. There is also a close relationship with the process of singing and of the songs themselves, which appears in poems such as *Josef Locke, Duende* and *I Will not Pity*. Finally, there is a constant tension of exploring the rawness of emotion which comes close to, but hopefully never crosses over, the line of sentiment.

John Fuller

How Far?

How far is it to Carcassonne?
I'll stir the dust until
I reach that glittering place I crave,
Heat-haunted citadel.

You were away before us,
With something on your mind,
Reckless of all horizon
And all you left behind.

Your friends of the cold morning,
The friends you lived among,
Who worked with you and fished with you
They heard you sing this song:

'How far is it to Carcassonne?
How difficult to find?
The years run on and on and on
Like waves upon the mind.'

How far is it to Carcassonne?
We sat at night alone.
I knew my heart was full enough.
The sea and shore were one.

You looked away. I heard you say:
'I'm going to Carcassonne.
My weary feet are stoutly shod,
My shoes are full of blood and bone
And while I have my breath, by God,
I'll go to Carcassonne.'

How far is it to Carcassonne?
How difficult to find?
The years run on and on and on
And I am left behind.

I see an endless highway
And an avenue of trees,
And the mind is truly lost among
Its own immensities.

I have a dream of something fine
That lives in towers of stone
And all those slaty turrets sing
This everlasting song.

How far is it to Carcassonne?
What life is left to run?
I do not have the years to spend
Upon these broken miles.

Although I do not see an end,
I do not have the patience left
To face blank stares with smiles,
For I shall soon be gone.

The skies are rent, the rock is cleft,
And we shall soon be dead.
How far is it to Carcassonne?
How far is it, how far?

How far is it to Carcassonne?
No trace of you is there,
Nor anywhere upon this road I tread,
Nor anywhere, nor anywhere.

Caroline Price

Messages

The war qualified you: you knew
the intricacies of circuits, coils and valves,
could clear a way through untuned fog,
the welter of the airwaves. You crouched close
to the shuddering floor, unreeling
the aerial, trawling it through the currents
like a weighted line.
                But he, defying
wires and metal, took pigeons up
with him, grey creatures tensed
against the capsules fastened to their legs
like amulets. At first in daylight,
releasing one each time
over the ubiquitous ocean, pale receding
specks of faith. Then at night: launching them
into wind or rain, convinced they'd run before him
back to base. Who needs your radio?
he bantered, stroking a recaptured bird,
pressing its softness to him,
anxious for a little warmth
before the emptiness,
the throbbing of another heart.

The Alde at Snape

I'm following my father along the river's bank,
the raised path squeezing between coils
of bramble – berries ripe,
he's calling back, for picking

and the reeds which whisper between creeks,
each taller than a man. The leaves'
keen cut, heads of maroon fronds
a shimmer of silk. Easy to think

that ribs were found here once, an Anglo-Saxon
burial ship, a claw beaker, a gold ring.
Treasures, still, are waiting to be discovered.
Never give up, I hear him say

but I'm struggling to keep him in sight
as the path twists, as masts and sails in the distance
turn to echo the river
like withies planted in the mud of the deepest water

to show the one navigable channel.
From here no guessing
the way ahead. As if in warning, the squeak
of a bird, invisible in the rushes

and the track stops abruptly,
like biting a thread: at my feet deep water welling,
a maverick flood from left to right
far too wide to leap,

only good for those who can balance
on grass blades, who can step along the length
of a single toppled reed
surely, from one place to another.

Clive Wilmer

A Blue Tit's Egg

Freckled like the brow
Of a pale child – beaked open to reveal
A fleck of yellow – no larger than my nail,
It was blown here on the wind.

Fledged or predated now,
The bird shrills in the thicket of my mind,
Unmindful how
Sturdy that first small crib was, yet how frail.

Learning to Read

in memory of my father

You were the man who named the birds
And, as you did so, taught me words –
Words on the page, that pinion there
Articulations of the air,

Much as the birds mark out their ground
With brilliant instances of sound.

The Translator's Apology

For Patrick McGuinness

I have been faithful to the text, after my own fashion.
There have been other adventures, other assignations,
Over and over, with words mouthed and whispered.
But I am faithful in spirit.
If I have gone astray,
If I have deviated into paraphrase,
If I have gone half-mad with imitation,
It has always been that some other dusky beauty
Reflected the original, a transitory embodiment.
Forgive me! Truth is my real goal.
Who that laid hands on that perfect form
Could do other than stay with that in perfect constancy?

Iain Britton

At the site of the future I light a fire...

warm my hands, scratch at my shadow leaning against a dry
crumpled stone. I'm
squatting,

staring at a sun spiked by the summits of Maungapohatu. In the bushes
birds sit, mesmerised by these flames.
Yesterday

you said you'd come back. You walked across the baked earth,
said you would be back – turned in the afternoon glare and
said it

and I believed it. In me you've become a
flicker of a thousand images, an ultramarine mirage
forming and reforming,

untouchable in spite of myself. In me I've this shape of a white-
painted figure coming in from the horizon of a desert. I'm
not alone. There's

another figure sticklike and identical and another and
another. It's not you who moves in single file, painted white and naked.
Not you. Not you. These men

hide nothing but their faces – eyes hooded and deep set -
I sense I know them, sense the liquefying fulfilment of their intrusion.
They warm their hands

by the fire too – one chants softly to himself – one prays to his stones,
another sings under his breath, while another
performs the miracle

of them being here with me. This is the living site of the future, this
cold before the sun clamps onto a lifting cloud – these hands
spread before the

desert fire of my making, this feeding of new shadows, my
overwhelming focus on the deaths of moths dashing into the flames,
my thoughts of you

still vivid but changing to a traveller gone off to a distant land. You
　said you'd
come back but I don't believe it'll happen any more. One day these
　men will
disappear too.

Ourselves Written in Wood

Hoofing up this hill with you
to this house of carvings, my
mind becomes a Namatjira

brainstorm of golden shimmers. Landscapes
turn over in their beds of fire,
bronze sculptures

grow upwards instead of trees. A
black man stands in solar spillage,
his body shining,

while green islands move like turtles
about his feet. The air
is packed with the stirred-up orbits

of people's faces. I feel them
crowd in. You kiss and
embrace them. Shake hands. The

air's heavy like water and our chests
heave in the stillness. You speak of
distances, the hard dried-out veins

of roads ... the bones, like piles of clothing,
left neatly in deserts, men and women
gone

chasing their afterlives. The house is
full of born-again hills and rivers and reusable
islands, it's full of languages

written in wood, animals rushing to
lusher pastures. In
this house, the night's a blind man.

Gradually, we lose sight of him, we
lose sight of objects, we lose sight
of ourselves.

Susan Wicks

Cat's Eye, Soft Shoulder

Each autumn we find we have forgotten
how dark dark is, how at only six
or five or even four, the mind-map of a town
folds in a web of creases, how lights suddenly explode
in our faces, seemingly unattached,
as if someone were questioning us with a torch
while behind the procession of twin beams
the hands and feet and features are sucked back
into shadows – how a familiar road
shrinks to a ribbon, snags and then unrolls
between cat's eye and soft shoulder
till even the way home
narrows one November evening to a lane
and what we used to think of as dark
was nothing, was only twilight, was a long game
played on into evening, where we stretched out our hands
and ran, sliding on dew-slick grass to meet the glimmer
of something falling, something that stung
and bounced off into brambles to lie here waiting
sodden, greyish, split open.

What do we do with spring

as we get older? How are we meant to cope
with all that sap rising, and the little birds
hopping from branch to branch,
all that inappropriate hope?

How are we supposed to react
to camellias, the shadow of leaves on grass, the young
taking their clothes off? How
do we keep intact
our skin of disbelief?

How keep our swollen joints
from knocking themselves frantic?
How close our ears and eyes and noses?
Tree pollen finds its way in.
Even with our eyes shut, we can taste roses.

French Kissing in Brittany

How could I have written this
at sixteen? The blue-grey fields
of artichokes to the horizon as I pedalled past
on a borrowed bike, my skin
welted with hives. And all those nights
as Cinderella while the two French girls
checked out the clubs, crashing back in at four a.m.
to rumple their bed with whispers.

Yet I still remember
the hunched shape of the blockhaus
built into the rock, the stones
beneath my spine, the grains of sand
still sticky from the tide, and at my feet
a glitter like sea-glass. It's well after midnight
and his mouth's a cave
as I grope for the entrance,
meteors falling at the corners of my eyes.

Stained Glass

Such colours in the window opposite –
ochre, forest, blue-grey –
the skin-tones of another kind of water.

In that room across the street,
a girl once woke to a ribbon of blood
unrolling across her bedspread; a young man ached
in forest green; a grandfather's jaw went slack
in a slate bandage. In an ochre lake
another baby got itself born.

Now the shape hunched over the joystick
of a Playstation is the same yellow
that knuckled a bony foot; the shadow
falling across a teenage magazine
once shivered in a ewer.
Nothing of what they see is theirs.

They are too late
for these borrowed colours, too soon
for the transparency of rain.

Lynn Roberts

Adonis

You must come, they said; he is hurt, they said.
My heart gave a kick like a growing child
and I ran – I ran down to the river,
running through the soft grasses and the sage brush
to him, lying there, lying on the bank.
He lay face down.
                    I did not like to move him,
though his poor face pressed into earth and thyme,
so I held his hand (it was cold and smooth
and slick, like altar candles) and I stroked
his thick black, long black hair. Bees vibrated
and the trees breathed; my sister Demeter
walked through the meadows with life in her train.

Let us take him, they said, to prepare him,
lady; and they raised him up in their arms.
His head fell back.
                    I watched them carry him
through the soft grasses and the sage brush, home.
Then I lay down in that little form where
the grass was flat and dark. And it was cold.

I looked to where the stars hid, and I felt
power surge in every cell, as though I might
inspire each last dead leaf and straw to love;
yet I had lost my own. Ichor ran like gold
under my skin, and under my hand blood
soaked the cool earth. Somewhere the boar cowered,
tusks as dark as wine.

Pat Earnshaw

Puppet without Strings

His body was a string of monkey-nuts.
Dressed in silk tunic
and trousers the colour of buttercups,
he hung from the brass candleholder
of the piano.

As arpeggios crashed
he nodded his head, his arms waved,
his legs danced.

His face
trailed black moustaches, he'd
slanting eyes, a pigtail of real hair.
His fluttering hands were paper claws.
They made me afraid.

A rainbow-tinted celluloid parrot, perched
on a ring, hung in the window, swung
in the wind.

A tin clown cycled past
on his tricycle. His clockwork legs
spun the wheel round. His mouth
grinned.

I too am jerked by cords,
by breezes from the window, wound-up
springs, by electronic bytes. A puppet,
losing control of motivating strings,
I jig to the incongruities of life.

Myra Schneider

Strawberries

                I

After the wild strawberry seeds sprouted
in a cupboard's warmth I coddled the spider stems
on a windowsill until I thought they could cope
with the garden where the unpredictable hums.
Now, revelling in freedom, they're multiplying

delicately serrated leaves up and down
my borders and opening hundreds of white-
petalled flowers whose firm centres
promise a summer of pitted pinkish fruits.
Kneeling on the path as if to pick a cupful

I'm twenty again, confused and intense,
searching under flowering currant bushes,
parting creeping violets from strawberry clumps.
As I watch myself peer into sun-grained rushes
of duskiness I come upon that moment

when the troubled, Crusade-weary knight
in Ingmar Bergman's *Seventh Seal* on a trail
to unravel meanings, rises from sleep
and, as he sits on the grass drinking the cool
of morning, is offered a bowl of strawberries

by the young wife in a travelling troupe.
It matters not that the film's in black and white –
what I take in is the girl's flaxen hair, moist
meadow green, the pink fragrance of the fruit,
a world healing as dock leaves laid on a wound.

II

It's May and the hedge parsley bordering the stream
in the park stands as tall as myself. I don't want
to dip into its dream layers but the decades
drop away and I'm cycling by verges pent
with white to the nursery where it took a week

to plant out the young strawberries, put up
cloches – tedious work. And for once
the wind isn't blowing in from the salt and sand
of the sea but out of the blue it pounces
on dozens of glistening lids, ferries them
across the field, then lets its victims go.
They crash onto unbroken glass, shatter.
The slow afternoon ripped, we line up, shaken,
by the unharmed greenhouse and stare at the clutter
of frames, the crushed fruit, the speckless sky.

Seven years later the shock that struck
from the blue was greater. Late on the last day
in Rome with my new husband, I read on a board
'Kennedy Assassinata.' As if the ground below
my feet was no longer reliable I began to tremble.

This May I touch unfathomable lacy grasses,
nurture the small berries and in the hope
of gathering a few ripe cupfuls I pull off
the snails clinging to stalks. Often I pick up
the word *safe*, ponder its precise meaning.

Nicholas Jagger

Das Nachtlied

My labile love cannot be stilled;
as night's net gathers lovers together,
my soul, a would-be lover,
swims and serenades in loneliness.

I live in my own hard light,
drinking returning flames
that break loose
from my fire storm;
every second reigning in
my fire-fecundity.

My proffered love
turns to indifference,
the work of giving without end.
Such sorry hands tire
with weight of bestowal,
the malleable clay of my heart
baked hard
by this love-effort labour.

Listen to the chattering springs
singing unseen,
the playfulness of couples
making this darkness their own.
What silver trickle of theirs
could gift to this grave soul...

Of bone and flame alone,
the celibate god
burns with phosphor brightness;
the charnel-house furnace within
sears the sentimental eye.

For what it dares not ask it hopes the more,
Yet still a famished love dies unfulfilled.

Moya Cannon

Starlings

Some things can't be caught in words,
starlings over an October river, for instance –
the way they lift from a roof-ridge in a cloud
directed by a hidden choreographer;
the way they rise, bank and fall,
tugging at some uncharted artery of the human heart;
the way the cloud tilts, breaks and melds
the undersides of wings garnering all the light
that's left in an evening sky;
the way they flow down onto a warehouse roof,
bird by brown bird.

Mc. Donald Dixon

Three Palms at Commerette

for Harold Simmons

Three palms swizzle the wind on this spit of land that
juts across the bay like rotten teeth, hanging from
gums that have forgotten pain. Roots entwine with shale,
brown like the brown bark, ringing with age on this slope.
Behind a shield of white-cassava leaves,
                                the cibonae takes shape.
His home is the gommiers' glade,
                                      between myriads
of green that haunt this coast. Green, the iguana's snare,
                                              man invades its space.

Your rain-soaked footprints wind across this broken ledge,
following the hill's hunched torso; a hunter close
to his kill. Your easel is the gloricedar's
           dying stump – Oh light! Its spectrum flares –

Colours uncurl from their virginal sheathes to greet
your tired bristles that have already smoothened
every curve, rebuilt every village, weaved every
seine, on this coast. Every smile dipped in turpentine
keeps your brushes supple to perform with youthful

zest. Memories pour from every waving cumulus
above the gray horizon as I stumble on
this spot. The middle palm is gone, but our two thieves
still hang side by side on their cross, here, on this
Golgotha. Stones clash, lightening indents the sky you
reduced in print on a piece of hardboard primed with
cerulean wash: Time is powerless to erase.

Fishermen no longer haunt this bay;
                              their hills of conch are gone.
Gone the merriment, the chirping slurp, the cauldron's
     boiling whelk. Gone too, the day's catch, no longer
frolicking in the surf as seines drag through black sand.
                Only death's subtle silence remains...

We remember you in our novenas,
                              in the pen's wake

raking through landscape after landscape, left unprimed,
     waiting for man's scourge. In the almond leaf's smile,
unblemished by hotel specks sullying the beach
and the bottle green print from the tourists' bikinis
     defacing our sand. You are gone and the pride
you taught us to wear on our foreheads even in
desolation wears thin like a flag grown tired
of its pole.
            I lament the changing of the guard,
the new conquistadores combing through your sacred
folds. Beauty lost is worthy of resurrection
though powerless to direct the tides. So, I nursed
a periwinkle back to life. Today it bore
its first white flower which I placed on your grave for
            your birthday, to keep the mind alive.

Biographies

Peter Abbs is Professor of Creative Writing at the University of Sussex. He is the author of seven volumes of poetry, including, most recently, *Viva La Vida*, published by Salt in 2005. His polemic against Post Modernism, *Against the Flow*, has been published recently by RoutledgeFalmer.

Timothy Adès is a translator-poet who tends to work with rhyme and metre. His awards include the John Dryden Prize and the Premio Valle-Inclán. His books to date are Victor Hugo's *How to be a Grandfather* from Hearing Eye and Jean Cassou's *33 Sonnets of the Resistance from Arc*.

Viv Apple has used her 70 years' life experience to colour her poems, from childhood during the Second World War, to working in a garage, office, library, as a primary school teacher – and as a mother and grandmother with such interests as volunteer driving, wildlife and sailing. Her poems have been widely published in poetry magazines.

Eavan Boland, born 1944 in Dublin, has received numerous awards for her writing. She divides her time between Dublin where she lives with her husband, the novelist Kevin Casey, and Stanford University, California where she is Bella Maybury and Eloise Maybury Knapp Professor in Humanities, and Melvin and Bill Lane Professor for Director of Creative Writing.

Alison Brackenbury's latest collection is *Bricks and Ballads* (Carcanet, 2004). New poems can be seen on her website, www.alisonbrackenbury.co.uk

Iain Britton is Director of Maori Studies at a large independent boys' school in Auckland, New Zealand. His poetry is published internationally in journals in the U.S. and the U.K., Australia and New Zealand.

Moya Cannon has published two collections of poems: *Oar* (Salmon Press, Galway 1990; Poolbeg Press, Dublin 1994 and Gallery Press, Meath 2,000), and *The Parchment Boat* (Gallery Press, 1997). A third collection, provisionally entitled *Carrying the Songs* is nearing completion. She has edited *Poetry Ireland Review* and is a member of Aosdána.

Ian Caws' current collection is *Taro Fair* (Shoestring Press). *The Canterbury Road* is due from Bluechrome this year.

Ruth Christie is a freelance translator of Turkish prose and poetry. Her most recent publication is *In the Temple of a Patient God*, poems by Bejan Matur (Arc Visible Poets 2004). With Richard McKane she has co-translated poems by Nazim Hikmet (Anvil Press, 2002). Their translations of the major Turkish poet, Oktay Rifat, will be published this year (Anvil Press).

Heather Coffey lives in Reading. She was born in 1940 in India and has been writing poetry since 1992. She has attended many courses in the Poetry School, London, and has worked under Tammy Yosseloff and Jane Draycott. Her poems have appeared widely, including in *South*, *Magma*, in *Entering the Tapestry*, a Poetry School anthology and in *Scintilla 10*.

David Cooke was born in Cheshire. He graduated in English from London University and worked for a number of years for the Poetry Library in London. His poems have appeared in numerous poetry magazines including *Poetry Wales*, *Orbis*, *Stand* and *Babel*.

Peter Dale's translation of Corbière, *Wry Blue Loves*, Anvil, 2006, received a Poetry Book Society Recommendation for Translation. A book-length interview, *Peter Dale in Conversation with Cynthia Haven*, appeared from Between the Lines Press in 2005. A booklet of his epigrams, *Eight by Five*, is due to appear this winter from Rack Press. He has also just finished for Anvil a translation of Paul Valéry's *Charmes and other poems*.

Lisa Dart was Lecturer in Education at the University of Sussex for ten years. She has published work on education, creativity and the imagination. Currently, she is Head of Curriculum Enhancement at St Bede's school and is completing her doctorate on poetry and post-modernism. She was runner-up in the international *Grolier Poetry Prize 2005* in the USA. Her debut pamphlet, *The Self in the Photograph*, was published by **The talllighthouse** last year.

John F. Deane's latest collection of poetry is *The Instruments of Art*, Carcanet 2006. He has published a book of essays: *In Dogged Loyalty: The Religion of Poetry, the Poetry of Religion* (Columba, 2006). He is the founder of Poetry Ireland and lives in Dublin.

Greg Delanty is Artist in Residence at St Michael's College, Vermont. His *Collected Poems* 1986-2006 came out this year from Carcanet. A supplement in *Agenda* for his 50th birthday in 2008 is planned for 2008.

Mc. Donald Dixon was born on October 1, 1944 in Castries, St. Lucia. He has been actively involved in the arts since the early 1960s and is well known as a writer and dramatist. His first collection of poems, *Pebbles*, was published in 1973. Other published works include: *The Poet Speaks*, 1981, *Season of Mist*, a novel, 2001 and *Collected Poems 1961-2001* in 2003. His work has appeared in journals in the U.S. and U.K. In 1993 he was awarded the St. Lucia Medal of Merit for his contribution to the arts.

Pat Earnshaw, a biologist and also an authority on antique laces, returned to creative writing in 1995. Her poetry publications include: *Pigeon Grounded* (1996), *Cychosis* (1997), *Out on a Limb* (1999), and a book of prose poems *My Cat Vince* (2000), all Gorse Publications. A pamphlet *The Golden Hinde* was published by Redbeck Press in 2002. Her pamphlet *Gothic Tales* was a Poetry Book Society Recommendation.

Robert Etty was born in Lincolnshire, where he still lives. His poetry has been widely published and his most recent collections are *Small Affairs on the Estate* (Pikestaff Press, 2000) and *The Blue Box* (Shoestring Press, 2001). *Half a Field's Distance: New and Selected Poems* is due from Shoestring Press in 2006.

John Fuller's recent volume of poems, *Ghosts* (Chatto and Windus), was shortlisted for the Whitbread Prize. His novel, *Flawed Angel*, was published last year, also by Chatto. His new collection, entitled *The Space of Joy* (Chatto) has a Poetry Book Society Recommendation. He has recently been awarded the Michael Braude Prize of the American Academy of Arts and Letters. He is an Emeritus Professor of Magdalen College, Oxford.

Sam Gardiner's collection *Protestant Windows* was published by Lagan Press in 2000. The title poem won the National Poetry Competition in 1993. In 2002 he received an Arts Council Writer's Award. His latest collection was published by Smith/Doorstep in 2004. He lives in Lincoln.

Matthew Geden was born and brought up in the English Midlands. He moved to Ireland in 1990 and runs his own bookshop, Bandon Books, in Bandon, Co. Cork. He distributes *Agenda* in Ireland. His poems have appeared in many magazines in Ireland and elsewhere. Lapwing published his *Kinsale Poems* in 1991 and his translations of Appolinaire in 2003. A new collection, *Swimming to Albania*, is forthcoming from Bradshaw Books.

John Greening's last collection was *The Home Key* (Shoestring). He has recently published studies of Yeats and First World War Poets with Greenwich Exchange. His next critical book will be about American poetry since 1963. His next collection of poetry is the result of a Society of Author's travel grant which took him to Iceland. He reviews for the TLS. His new website is www.johngreening.co.uk

Harry Guest's *Collected Poems*, entitled *A Puzzling Harvest*, appeared from Anvil in 2002. His third novel *Time After Time* was published by Albertine Press last November.

Robert Hamberger's collections are: *Warpaint Angel* (Blackwater, 1997) and *The Smug Bridegroom* (Five Leaves, 2002). He was chosen for the Alternative Generation promotion, was awarded a Hawthornden Fellowship and shortlisted for a Forward prize. In spring 2007 a third collection *Torso* is due from Redbeck and *Heading North* is due from Flarestack.

Michael Hamburger is perhaps the most highly acclaimed translator of German Poetry. Among his many works of translation are the poetry of Rilke and Hölderlin. He has also written several critical books on translation and poetry. He has won acclaim for his own poetry and is devoting the remainder of his years to his own work. He lives in Suffolk with his wife, the poet Anne Beresford.

Marc Harris was born in 1962 in Cardiff. He spent 30 years living in England but returned to Wales in 2000 and now works with homeless people in Cardiff. His poems, which have won prizes, have been widely published in the UK, Ireland, the US and New Zealand.

John Haynes has published three volumes of poetry, *Sabon Gari* (London Magazine Editions) and *First the Desert Came and then the Torturer* (under the name of Idi Bukar: RAG Press, Nigeria). His latest book is a long poem, *Letter to Patience* (Seren), set mainly in Nigeria in 1993. For eighteen years he worked at Ahmadu Bello University, Zaria, Nigeria where he met and married his Nigerian wife. They have two children. He has also written on African poetry, and fiction for African children, along with the usually scholarlies. He now lives in Hampshire.

Stuart Henson's most recent collections are *Ember Music* (Peterloo, 1994) and *A Place Apart* (Shoestring, 2004). A selection of his work also appeared in the *Oxford Poets 2002* Anthology.

Nicholas Jagger is an artist and poet living in Yorkshire. Work in progress includes a series of impromptus based on Nietzche's *Also Sprach Zarathustra*, which he hopes to complete by the end of 2007.

Judith Kazantzis has published nine collections of poetry including her *Selected Poems*. Her latest collection is *Just After Midnight (*Enitharmon 2004). She was Royal Literary Fund Fellow at Sussex University 2005-6. Her novel *Of Love And Terror* came out in 2002, together with her Odyssean translation, *In Cyclops' Cave*. She lives in Lewes and also makes prints. See www.writersartists.net

Mimi Khalvati has published five collections with Carcanet, including her *Selected Poems* (2000) and *The Chine* (2002). She is the founder of The Poetry School. She currently holds a Royal Literary Fund Fellowship at City University and will be the William Quarton Fellow at the International Writing Program in Iowa this year. She received a Cholmondeley Award in 2006 and a new collection, *The Meanest Flower*, is forthcoming in 2007.

John Kinsella is the author of many books of poetry – published by Bloodaxe, Salt and Norton – for which he has been highly praised. He divides his time between the US, Australia (where he was brought up) and England. He is a Fellow of Churchill College, Cambridge University, Professor of English at Kenyon College where he edits the American journal, *The Kenyon Review*, and Adjunct Professor to Edith Cowan University. His latest collections, *Peripheral Light: New and Selected Poems*, and *The New Arcadia: Poems*, both published by Norton were reviewed by Martin Dodsworth in the previous issue of ***Agenda***: *Poems on Water*, Vol. 42 No.1 (£8).

Michael Kinsella lives in Northern Ireland. He is a freelance writer and reviewer and is currently writing a piece on crushes.

Michael Kirkham, born and educated in England, has lived and worked in Canada since 1968. He is Professor Emeritus in English at the University of Toronto. His books include *The Poetry of Robert Graves* (1969), *The Imagination of Edward Thomas* (1986) and *Passionate Intellect: The Poetry of Charles Tomlinson* (1999).

Mark Leech's most recent book of translations, *Anglo Saxon Voices*, is published by Pipers' Ash Ltd. He has had poems published in a wide range of magazines. He organises and performs at poetry events in Oxford.

Sally Lucas has had poems published in various magazines and has appeared in a few anthologies.

Malcolm MacClancy (b.1967) is from Co. Clare in the West of Ireland. His poetry has been published widely and he has won the *Patrick McGill Poetry Prize*. He writes lyrics with *Interference* (www.interference.ie), a cult band described by RTE as 'almost mythical, definitely legendary'. He has worked as a market-trader, teacher, journalist and film-maker. Most recently he has been managing a shelter for homeless people in Dublin.

Tom MacIntyre was born in Cavan, Ireland in 1931. He has written plays for the Abbey Theatre in Dublin, and a novel, *Story of a Girl* (Lilliput, 2000). He is an established poet. One of his collections, *Stories of The Wandering Moon,* came out from Lilliput in 2000.

Johnny Marsh was born in 1961 in Sussex. He studied Fine Art at Goldsmiths College in London. He lives in Sussex and works in a Children's Home, and as an agricultural labourer. He is currently training at Goldsmiths to be an Art Therapist and works a few days a week in a psychiatric ward of a hospital.

Sam Milne lives and works in Surrey, although his heart resides in Aberdeen. He is currently writing a long essay on the Scots dialect-writer Flora Garry who writes in Broad Buchan, his own native language. He has just written a novel which is looking for a publisher, and has completed a study on Marcel Proust which will be included in his forthcoming book of collected essays. He is also updating his critical study on the poetry of Geoffrey Hill. He has no regrets about retiring from teaching!

Steven O'Brien grew up singing. His Welsh and Irish family were all conjurors of song. His primal poetic touchstones are the towering hymns of Wales and the muscular ballads of Ireland. He lives in Worthing and lectures in Creative Writing at the University of Portsmouth. His first full-length collection, *Dark Hill Dreams*, was published by **Agenda Editions** this year.

William Oxley's poetry was the subject of a book-length study *The Romantic Imagination* from Poetry Salzburg in 2005. An illustrated booklet of his *Poems Antibes* will be launched at the end of this year at the English Bookshop in Antibes.

Geraldine Paine gained an M.Phil in Writing at the University of Glamorgan in 2000. Her poems have been published in *The Rialto, The Shop, Magma, Envoi, Soundings, The Interpreter's House, Seam, Smith's Knoll, Connections, Equinox,* the e-zine wanderingdog.com, and the Kent and Sussex Competition Anthology 2000.

Jay Parini is a poet, novelist and biographer. His biography of Robert Frost won the Chicago-Tribune Heartland Award in 2000. In 2005, he published his fifth volume of poetry: *The Art of Subtraction: New and Selected Poems* (Braziller). He teaches in Vermont at Middlebury College, where he has recently returned from a spell of living in London.

Simon Pomery was born in Galway in 1982, and grew up in Buxton, Derbyshire. He was educated at Leeds University and Pembroke College, Cambridge. His work has been published, or is forthcoming, in *Poetry London, Anon, Poetry and Audience,* and *P.N. Review*. He currently lives in Fife.

Caroline Price is a violinist and teacher living in Kent. Her most recent publications are

Pictures against Skin (Rockingham Press) and, as co-editor, *Four Caves of the Heart*, an anthology of 14 women poets (Second Light Publications). She is currently preparing a new collection for Shoestring.

Lynn Roberts read English at Bedford College, University of London, after which she studied Art History at the Courtauld Institute. She is a picture frame historian and prize-winning poet.

Tony Roberts is currently an assistant head in a Bolton comprehensive school. He has published *Flowers of the Hudson Bay* (Peterloo Poets) and *Sitters* (Arc). His work has appeared widely in the literary press.

Linda Saunders's first full-length book of poems, *Ways of Returning* (Arrowhead Press), was shortlisted last year for the Jerwood Aldeburgh First Collection Prize. Her poetry has been widely published in magazines and anthologies, including *New Women Poets* (Bloodaxe), and a chapbook, *She River*, from Vane Women Press.

Tania van Schalkwyk, 32, was born in Africa and raised in Arabia and America. She has had 37 homes on various continents and now lives in Cape Town, South Africa. Her poems have been published in many magazines, and broadcast widely in the UK, Germany and South Africa. She is also an artist.

Myra Schneider's most recent poetry collections are *Multiplying the Moon* (Enitharmon 2004) and *Insisting on Yellow, New and Selected Poems* (Enitharmon 2000). Her book *Writing My Way Through Cancer* (Jessica Kingsley 2003) is a fleshed-out journal with poem notes and poems. She has co-edited four anthologies of poetry by contemporary women poets, most recently: *Images of Women* (Arrowhead 2006). She is a core tutor for the Poetry School.

Duncan Sprott's most recent novel is *Daughter of the Crocodile* (Faber, 2006), the second instalment of *The Ptolemies Quartet*. He lives in County Cork, Ireland.

Robert Stein's poems have appeared in ***Agenda*** previously, as well as in *Poetry Review*, *Ambit*, *The Rialto*, *Envoi*, *Orbis* and *The Wolf*. He reviews contemporary classical music for *International Record Review* and *Tempo*.

Daniel Tobin is the author of three books of poems, *Where the World is Made*, winner of the Bakeless Prize, *Double Life*, and *The Narrows*, which was a finalist for the Forward Poetry Book of the Year Award and a featured book on *Poetry Daily*. His fourth book of poems, *Second Things*, is forthcoming from Four Way Books in 2008. Among his awards are the "The Discovery/*The Nation* Award," The Robert Penn Warren Award, the Robert Frost Fellowship, and a creative writing fellowship from the National Endowment for the Arts. Widely published in journals in the United States and abroad, his work also has been anthologized in *The Bread Loaf Anthology of New American Poets*, *Hammer and Blaze*, *The Norton Introduction to Poetry*, and elsewhere. He is chair of the Department of Writing, Literature, and Publishing at Emerson College in Boston.

Richard Marggraf Turley, 35, lectures in English Literature and Creative Writing at the University of Wales, Aberystwyth. His co-authored first collection, *Whiteout*, is forthcoming with Parthian Books in 2007.

Susan Wicks has published five collections, as well as two novels and a short memoir. Her most recent book of poems, *De-iced*, is to be published by Bloodaxe in January 2007. She is the Director of the Centre for Creative Writing at the University of Kent in Canterbury.

Clive Wilmer is a poet and lecturer, who lives and teaches in Cambridge. His most recent collection is *The Mystery of Things* (Carcanet, 2006).